Like many, I first met the Puritans [illegible] and thus owe him a debt of grat[illegible] has once again excelled: here are thoughtful introductions to some key Puritan thinkers and their works, along with a Puritan manifesto for today's pastors. This is vintage Packer. In an age of trendy fluff, here is solid food for the church and for the soul.

Carl R. Trueman
Paul Woolley Professor of Church History,
Westminster Theological Seminary, Philadelphia, Pennsylvania

When I've been asked to recommend a book on the Puritans, J. I. Packer's *A Quest for Godliness* typically came first to mind. With the release of *Puritan Portraits,* a fresh and spiritually invigorating survey of several key Puritan pastors and theologians, I can now point to a second volume that is must reading. 'Puritan Christianity', says Packer, 'was serious business.' So, too, must ours be, and there is simply no better tour guide for exploring Puritan faith and spirituality than J. I. Packer. Highly recommended!

Sam Storms
Senior Pastor,
Bridgeway Church, Oklahoma City, Oklahoma

With characteristic ease of style, clarity of thought, and theological insight, Dr Packer introduces us to the life and thought of seven of the all-time masters of what one of them called 'The Life of God in the Soul of Man'. *Puritan Portraits* is a treat for anyone with healthy spiritual taste buds.

Sinclair B. Ferguson
Senior Minister,
First Presbyterian Church, Columbia, South Carolina

The best way to meet great men is through a personal introduction by someone who knows them well. That's precisely what J. I. Packer does in this book, introducing us to several Puritan-minded men of the sixteenth through eighteenth centuries. But this is more than biography. As Packer does so well, in this book the Puritans become mirrors in which we see heavenly truths about the gospel, evangelism, spiritual growth, and suffering. I thank God for the gathering of this previously scattered material into one volume, and anticipate that it will bless many.

Joel R. Beeke
President,
Puritan Reformed Theological Seminary, Grand Rapids, Michigan

Over the years, J. I. Packer has convinced many of us that, if we would be more than spiritual pygmies, we need to spend time with the Puritans. Now, in this elegant and engaging book, he has given us the most accessible and inspiring way in to them. Thank you, Dr Packer, thank you!

Michael Reeves
Head of Theology, UCCF
Oxford, England

J.I. Packer has a skill unparalleled in today's church: he brings the Puritans back to life and makes them sing, as the biographical expositions in this book attest. Indeed, Jim Packer is a Puritan of the most winsome, persuasive, and catholic sort. When young ministers ask me what they should study to strengthen their spiritual life, I often say, 'Read the Puritans with Packer!' That is good counsel for all Christians.

Timothy George
General Editor of the *Reformation Commentary on Scripture,*
Founding Dean,
Beeson Divinity School of Samford University, Birmingham, Alabama

Puritan Portraits

J.I. Packer on Selected Classic Pastors and Pastoral Classics

Richard Baxter
Thomas Boston
John Bunyan
Stephen Charnock
John Flavel
Matthew Henry
John Owen
William Perkins
Henry Scougal

J.I. Packer

Christian Focus

J. I. Packer is named by *Time* Magazine as one of the 25 most influential evangelicals alive. He is the Board of Governor's Professor of Theology at Regent College, Vancouver, BC, Canada.

paperback ISBN 978-1-84550-700-8
epub ISBN 978-1-78191-075-7
Mobi ISBN 978-1-78191-076-4

Published in 2012
by
Christian Focus Publications,
Geanies House, Fearn,
Ross-shire, IV20 1TW, Great Britain.
www.christianfocus.com

Cover design by Paul Lewis

Printed by
Bell and Bain, Glasgow

CONTENTS

Prologue

If today you acquire a book that announces itself as a devotional, or has been marketed as such, you do not expect to find it made up of expository sermons and essays, both doctrinal and historical. Books with such contents do not call themselves devotionals, and self-styled devotionals ordinarily consist of meditations and prayers on aspects of daily life, and no more. Is there anything odd about this? I suggest there is.

Reflected here, as it seems to me, is the slimmed-down, man-centred idea of devotion to God that has currently become all too common. Like much more of the historic Christian vocabulary, devotion is a cheapened word nowadays, and a secularised one into the bargain. We speak freely of devotion to a cause, or to one's spouse or children, or to one's work, but it is rare to hear of devotion to God. Why is that? Is it that we are not devoted to God as our forebears were, or that we conceal our devotion in a way that our predecessors did not? Whatever the reason, the fact is there, and our idea of devotion appears foreshortened. Once it signified adhering to God, the Father, the Son and the Spirit, in loyalty and love with all one's heart, mind, soul and strength; a single-minded concentration on praising and pleasing God as our life's key activities. And included in the understanding of devotion was an appetite for learning wisdom from didactic study and exposition of Scripture. In former days, preaching and devotion were seen as correlates – faithful Bible teaching fed hearers with truth to trust, digest, and live out, and faithful Christians looked for, and longed for, didactic displays of biblical thought and teaching by which to shape their self-management in both living with God and relating to family, friends, colleagues and other human beings.

Examples of expository ministry with a devotional direction, such as was once desired and appreciated, include the preaching of C.H. Spurgeon, who during his forty-year concentration on setting forth the saving grace of Christ covered just about everything in Christian doctrine, ethics and spiritual life; Matthew Henry's written exposition of the Bible, garnished with shrewd practical observations of all sorts; and many more of the Puritans' homiletic products, samples of which are introduced in the following pages.

Would we refer to Spurgeon's sermons, or Matthew Henry's massives volumes, or Stephen Charnock's supersize sermons on *The Existence and Attributes of God*, or the extended expositions of any other Puritan writer, as devotionals? I doubt whether many of us would, but I think that all of us should; for, in my understanding of devotion, that is what they really are. I ask my readers to think from the outset of the Puritans as writers of devotionals, and I hope by the end of the book to have convinced you that is truly is so. And if, in fact, this book of mine came to be thought of as itself a devotional introducing other devotionals and their authors, no one would be more pleased than I.

J.I. Packer
May 2012

Part I:

Puritan Pastors at Work

Puritan Pastors at Work

I

This book centres upon Puritan clergy and their message. But why, it may at once be asked, should any of that be of interest to us today? The Puritans were arrogant, strait-laced bigots, were they not? And the Puritan era (roughly, a century and a half, 1560 to 1710) was long ago and far away, many moons before industrial technology and, more recently, information technology took over the ordering of civilised life; how then can a voice from so distant a past be of help to us now? It is not as if any element of Puritanism changed Western society in a permanently decisive way; on the contrary, Puritanism as popularly perceived and as a Western cultural memory is currently a reference point for a hidebound, restricted, inhibited way of life that ever since the end of the seventeenth century the West has explicitly rejected – isn't that so? Is it not then the simple truth that Puritanism, whatever it may or may not have been, is an historical episode best forgotten and that Puritan religion, however well-meant in its time, should be judged irrelevant to modern life?

Well, no. Proverbial wisdom warns us against letting the baby flow away with the bath-water, but that is what most evangelical Christianity has done with its Puritan heritage over the past three centuries, and the results are distinctly unhappy. No doubt there was a good deal of Puritan bath-water needing to be emptied, but the essential Puritan insight into the Christian life as a blend of structured obedience and hope based on freedom in and through Christ and on promises of grace sustaining close communion with God was a precious synthesis that Christians should have prized, and sadly did not. Clergy should have taught it, and sadly did not. So at this point we live in a vacuum today, and it shows. Many ministers are unclear as to what they should tell their congregations about holiness and godliness, and many church people are quite lost when it comes to the specifics of spelling out, commending and living the Christian life. These are shortcomings which a grasp of the heart of Puritanism would cure.

The following pages embody the belief that as Isaac re-dug his father Abraham's wells which the Philistines had filled in (Gen. 26:18), so we today need to re-dig the wells of Puritan wisdom regarding gospel truth, gospel grace, and gospel life. My plan is to introduce some of the most distinguished teachers of these things. But, to provide a frame for their convictional portraits, I need to begin by sketching out the dynamic reality of which they were part, namely, the Puritan movement as such.

First, let it be said that those who identified with this movement did not call themselves Puritans nor welcome the label when others applied it to them, for it sounded in their ears as what it seems originally to have been – namely, an insult, a term of abuse, implying such censorious Pharisaism as Shakespeare's Sir Toby Belch detected in Malvolio, along with a lack of loyalty to the Church of England and a hidden wish to separate from it. Beyond 'the godly' and 'the brethren' these zealous souls had no names either for the movement itself or for themselves as part of it. What they did was form informal, ginger-group networks, united by knowing that the furtherance of God's kingdom in

England, and His glory thereby, was what they all were after. Preaching, prayer, 'conference' between themselves on kingdom topics, ordered family life, and Sabbatarianism, marked them out. All walks of life were represented in their clergy-led ranks, all active one way or another in the pursuit of their common goals. Their activism commanded attention, and gave rise to much hostility among those who did not share their goals. But it is hardly too much to say that for 100 years, from 1560 to 1660, it was the Puritan movement that made most of the running in England's religious life.

The movement had two areas of concern and action. One was the organisational set-up of the Church of England, from its *Book of Common Prayer* to its episcopal hierarchy; all of which Puritans wanted to bring into line with what other Reformed churches did, and none of which Elizabeth, the Church's titular head, was prepared to have changed. The second and larger concern was the converting of England to a vital evangelical faith, which they thought could be achieved through effective ministry in the parishes. Most of the brethren seem to have been concerned about both agendas, but active chiefly in one. In this book, the second is our concern.

Elizabethan England was mainly rural and many of the worshippers in its several thousand parishes were illiterate. A tenacious religious conservatism, harking back to pre-Reformation days, was widespread and attitudes towards the current religious settlement were on the whole cool and detached. Yet, providentially as we may think, England's culture had in it a deep sense of the reality of the holy God who impacts every life; of the authority of the Bible, long locked up in Latin but now available in English for anyone motivated to read it; and of the authority of the clergyman as preacher and teacher, should he choose to fulfil these roles (not all clergy did). Also, church attendance was required by law. All this gave Puritan pastors a large launch-pad from which to take off in their pastoral endeavours.

By the turn of the sixteenth century, the church-reform activists in the movement had effectively shot their bolt.

Energetic clerical propagandists had campaigned with vigour for the revision or abolition of the Prayer Book, Presbyterian church order countrywide, freedom to not use ceremonies that in their view tended to maintain unbelief, and public funding for ministerial trainees at the universities. They had tried to establish local Bible teaching meetings ('prophesyings') as a regular part of church life, and, wisely or unwisely, some had joined in a venture to see what satirizing the hierarchy might do (the Marprelate tracts). And they had lost every battle they fought. Now they lacked resources, energy and morale for further fighting. But as reformism wound down discipling endeavours had begun to take off. The torch had been lit in 1570, when a young don named Richard Greenham had chosen to leave Cambridge and become vicar of Dry Drayton, a country parish just outside the city. The high standards of ministry that Greenham maintained as preacher, pastor and personal counsellor had caught imaginations and made his name something of a household word in East Anglia. Also, he had developed an apprenticeship system for ministerial students, who lived with him and learned their trade by involvement in his work, under his direct supervision; then they took his wisdom with them into pastoral posts of their own.

Thus Greenham, as we say, had started something, and others were beginning to make the same sort of waves as he did. One of his students, Henry Smith, became a devotional preacher who for years was the talk of London. Meantime, a Cambridge contemporary, William Perkins, a learned godly man with a flair for speed and clarity as a writer, began in the 1580s a long series of practical devotional books to lead ordinary people into living the life of faith in Jesus Christ. These filled a gap; nothing like them had existed before, and they sold widely, thus establishing the Puritan principle that a helpful, desirable and indeed necessary habit for literate believers was to read 'good books,' as they were called. The vision of a literature covering all aspects of the Christian life caught on, and in that pre-dust-jacket age individual title-pages reflected it. Thus, in 1603 Richard Rogers published a folio announcing itself as *Seven Treatises, Containing*

Such Directions as is gathered out of the holie Scriptures, leading and guiding to true happiness, both in this life and in the life to come; and may be called the practice of Christianitie, profitable for all such as heartily desire the same; in the which, more particularly true Christians may learne how to leade a godly and comfortable life every day (8th ed., 1630). In a surprisingly short time Puritanism created for itself a whole library of smaller instruction books, usually courses of sermons now written up for the press, covering doctrinally and homiletically all the many aspects of the warrior-pilgrim Christian life as Puritanism understood it, and as Bunyan classically pictured it in *Pilgrim's Progress*. When in 1673, in his massive *Christian Directory*, Richard Baxter set himself to recommend 'the poorest or smallest library that is tolerable' for a preacher, he named fifty-eight 'affectionate practical English writers' and urged the would-be preacher to collect their works – 'as many as you can get.' 'Affectionate' here meant, arousing motivational feelings through the use of imagination and dramatic rhetoric; 'practical' meant, as it means today, making clear what should be believed and done. It was the popular Christian literature on doctrine, duty and devotion which Puritanism had produced that Baxter was recommending, and it is through this literature that we today are able to appreciate the special excellence of Puritan pastoral ministry.

II

Puritan Christianity was serious business: witness Richard Rogers's reply to the lord of the manor's complaint that his religion was over-precise – 'O sir, I serve a precise God.' Many Puritans, lay and clerical, journalled in order to achieve inner honesty, avoid self-deception in spiritual things, and keep close to God. Puritan pastors took their calling very seriously: witness the plaque that stood on William Perkins's study table, thus inscribed: 'Thou art a Minister of the Word: Mind thy business.' And Puritan pastors were down-to-earth realists in fulfilling their responsibilities to the members of their congregations. Salvation in Christ through faith for each one was their goal, and they shaped their parochial strategy to this end. They put their preaching of the gospel first, because they believed that in God's economy this was the prime means of the grace by which God saves souls; but they buttressed their preaching ministry with catechizing on the one hand and counselling on the other, and thus made it immeasurably stronger in its impact.

Catechizing was for them a distinct discipline of teaching basic Christian beliefs by question and answer. In the sixteenth and seventeenth centuries all Protestant church leaders were agreed that catechizing from childhood through adulthood was an essential element in church life, without which the church could hardly survive, or hope to survive. The syllabus of virtually all catechisms from that era centres upon the doctrines of the Apostles' Creed, the duties indicated by the Ten Commandments, and the parameters of prayer, according to the pattern set forth in the Lord's Prayer. The Prayer Book of the Church of England had in it a children's catechism that clergy, along with parents and godparents, were required to teach, and children were required to learn before being confirmed and entering into the Church's communicant life. Also, after 1570, as tools for further instructing teens and adults in the basics of faith and practice, the Church had available both longer and shorter versions of a fuller, semi-official catechism by Alexander Nowell. In addition to these resources, however, Puritan clergy used an abundance of orthodox catechisms of their own devising, which shows how necessary and important they took competent catechizing to be. For faith, to the Puritans, started with factual knowledge – knowledge of who and what God is, who and what Jesus Christ is, and what the gospel is – and the purpose of catechizing was to open the door to the life of faith by laying faith's cognitive foundations.

Counselling, to use the modern word that covers what they were doing, was a form of one-on-one ministry which the Puritans described as 'comforting afflicted consciences'. They meant by this giving troubled souls help in a way analogous to the physician's service to one who is weak or sick: that is, diagnosing what is wrong and prescribing the way to bring about a cure. For this, the pastor needed a knowledge of spiritual pathology, the malfunctioning of the soul under both the external and internal pressures to which it may be exposed; and for that, he needed to be clear from the start on what constituted inward spiritual health. The Puritans grasped the New Testament notion of spiritual health – Christ-centred faith, hope and love expressed in good works; assurance, peace, and joy; a heart and mind constantly engaged in praise and thanksgiving; and zeal for God's kingdom and glory, leading to purposeful and energetic action. Spiritual malaise, by contrast, appeared in doubt, despair, fear, hatred, apathy, tormenting temptations to allow oneself bad habits; lack of courage, of backbone, and of zeal; pride, lust, greed, bitterness, discontent, self-absorption, self-pity, irresolution and indiscipline and such like. The various modes of what we today call depression, for which the rough equivalent during the Puritan years was melancholy, also raised their heads either separately from, or together with, the failings listed above.

The Puritan resources for restoring these spiritual sufferers to peace, hope, joy and renewed energy to serve God were, first, deep empathy with and insight into their inward distresses, in their physical and mental as well as their directly spiritual dimensions; second, deep understanding both of the radical corruption of fallen human nature, which makes meritorious action impossible and of God's free grace in Christ, who by dying absorbed sin's guilt and now in risen power rescues sinners from sin's perverting effects in their lives; third, deep perception of the ways of God, whereby in and through Christ He restores His image in us, and the ways of Satan, who by every means in His power seeks to keep us from enjoying the life of God with God here and hereafter; and fourth, shrewd clarity about the lineaments of true and false religion, as both were being practised in England during the Puritan era. The pastors saw themselves as set in place by God to help needy souls keep clear of Satan's control, its allurements notwithstanding, and to stay under God's control, despite the temporary pressures and pains of doing so. The recognition and renunciation of unbelief and disobedience, the constant practice of fellowship and praise, with avoidance of self-absorption and solitariness, and regular returning to God's promises in Scripture, were the basic formula for the afflicted soul's recovery: the pastors, as wise spiritual physicians, would ring the changes on it as particular cases of distress required. In all of this Richard Greenham was both the pioneer and the pundit, whose example, method, and success rate led to his being treated as a model by an entire generation of Puritan counsellor-pastors.

On the third and fourth of the resources listed above, something more needs to be said.

The pastors' vivid sense of ongoing conflict between Satan and the triune God within each believer led them to picture the Christian life as very often and very much a battlefield, on which God was always manoeuvring to make sure that His child heeded His commands, promises and warnings, while Satan endlessly counter-manoeuvred in hope of blunting the impact of God's words by distortion or distraction, and eventually of reclaiming the sinner whom God by regeneration had wrenched from his grasp. The trouble of the troubled souls regularly revolved round uncertainty as to whether they would finally be saved; the proof that they were among God's chosen and called, who would be kept safe till they reached heaven, was that they wanted God's forgiveness through Christ for the past and they wanted to live lives of godliness in the present and for the future; and the best help the pastor could give them was to enable them to discern and embrace the change that God had already wrought in them, and to focus their determination, come hell or high water, to live it out consistently.

By false religion the Puritans meant, in general, any and every combination of external observances and superstitious beliefs that did not lead to faith-fellowship with God through Christ or to inner regenerative transformation by the indwelling

Holy Spirit. When they spoke of false religion, however, they regularly had in mind Roman Catholicism as they knew it, or thought they knew it, as the great exemplar of what they were talking about. A good deal of popular Papistry, to use their word, still survived as a mind-set at grass roots level in rural England, and it should not surprise us that anti-Papistry was a note that Puritan preachers – like other English preachers, only more stridently – often struck. Rightly or wrongly, Puritans generally saw the Roman Catholic Church as embodying the principle of justification by meritorious works, and denounced it on this basis. Like Luther, they believed that justification by works is fallen mankind's natural religion, which everyone needs to be directly winkled out of if ever they are to appreciate the saving grace of Jesus Christ the Lord.

III

It has been said that the essence of tragedy is waste of good, both actual and potential, and by this definition the demise of Puritanism was tragedy in its purest form. It had truly been a movement: that is, an association of people banded together and active to bring about some form of change for what they saw as the better. Puritanism was for a century, as we have seen, a headline-hitting holiness movement on two fronts: under Elizabeth, mainly a quest for pure worship through a purging of the Anglican church order; under James I and Charles I, mainly a quest for godly parochial communities; through the Civil War and under the Commonwealth, a quest for both goals together. But when the English monarchy and the Church of England returned at the Restoration, the Puritan movement was deliberately and systematically snuffed out by governmental action. The reason, no doubt, was officialdom's understandable fear of renewed civil unrest; the effect, however, was to demolish in twenty-five years what the Puritans had spent 100 years building. Public opinion, egged on from the top, swung against the Puritans, viewing them as disruptive eccentrics and greeting the return of the old order with joy and relief. The

1662 Act of Uniformity required all clergy who would serve within re-established Anglicanism to abjure rebellion against the king in all its forms (that included, of course, retrospective condemnation of the Parliamentary cause in the Civil War, which many clergy had backed); with that, to declare that the Book of Common Prayer, now slightly revised (though not as the Puritans wanted), needed no further change; and also to receive episcopal ordination if they did not have it already. (It had not been available since Anglicanism was abolished in 1645.) Nearly two thousand Puritan pastors could not in conscience accept all this, and so perforce vacated their parish ministries. Further Parliamentary legislation then restricted their movements and forbade them to gather congregations of their own, while forbidding layfolk to join such congregations in any case. Over a period of twenty and more years some twenty thousand Puritans, mostly layfolk, saw the inside of gaols for breaches of these enactments. This was the last period of religious persecution in England, and its length made it the worst.

When in 1689, William of Orange having become England's king, the Toleration Act was passed, the Puritan constituency had lost its power to be a movement in any meaningful sense and became a mixed bag of independent nonconformist congregations scattered up and down the country, marginal both to the Church of England and to England's national life.

One of the marginalising factors was the exclusion from Oxford and Cambridge, the two English universities, of students who would not profess the same wholesale assent to the restored Church of England as was required of its clergy. Some of 1662's ejected clergy, however, opened schools, and out of these grew academies that matched university standards and could offer a full academic preparation for pastoral ministry. Through this source of supply of pastors, nonconformist church life became sturdily self-sustaining, in parallel to, though wholly separate from, the Anglican parish network that covered the country. It is a fact, arguably an unhappy one, that when the great renewal of godly Christian experience under Whitefield and the Wesleys took hold in the 1730s nonconformists were deeply suspicious of it, doubted its stability and stood largely aloof from it. They were, however, able to keep themselves going without revivalist help.

IV

Puritanism's most significant contribution to the ongoing life of the church was, and is, without doubt its literary legacy. As has been already indicated, Puritans appreciated both the power of the press and England's need for devotional reading, and those of their number with writing skills laboured hard after the turn of the sixteenth century to supply that need. The pioneer was William Perkins, but he had no lack of followers. We now round off our sketch of Puritan pastors at work with some discussion of this mass of material.

The first thing to say is that since the mid-nineteenth century, spasmodically perhaps but with recurring enthusiasm from one and another, the church has been generously provided with Puritan reprints. Richard Baxter, John Owen, Thomas Goodwin, Richard Sibbes, Stephen Charnock, John Bunyan, Thomas Manton, John Flavel, William Gurnall, John Howe and Matthew Henry, are among the authors whose works have been made available to us in modern dress. The reprinters have regularly seen it as part of their job to sanitise the material orthographically and grammatically, and though this forfeits surface-level authenticity it makes these Puritans a great deal easier to read, so we should be grateful that it has been done.

These full editions make possible something not possible before, namely assessment of each writer's total output, and of key themes permeating it, and substantive cross-references within it – tempting raw material for doctoral dissertations, of course, and in fact many such are nowadays written.

Valuable as this kind of study is, however, it overshadows the fact that most of the writing is occasional, the work of men for whom it was, if not exactly a spare-time activity, then at least an incidental item in a life in which preaching the gospel, caring for a congregation, and responding to pastoral emergencies, came first. Puritan pastors were not professional authors, but saw the writing they did as essentially back-up for, and sometimes extension of, their ongoing ministry to living souls.

The second thing to say is that the bulk of Puritan devotional writing appears on inspection to be lightly edited versions of material that was first written for the pulpit. All preachers in Elizabeth's Church of England (to start there) were expected to write out and memorise each sermon, so that delivering it would actually be a recitation, comparable to an actor speaking his lines. Any passion in its delivery would be a thing of the moment, but what was delivered was not of the moment; it was, rather, a precomposed and now remembered speech. Puritan preachers never challenged this convention, though clearly under certain circumstances they bypassed it. Thus, Greenham at Dry Drayton, so we are told, preached at six on each of five mornings weekly, rising at four to prepare, and when he felt strongly about his topic he could get muddled in the pulpit; evidently, then, he preached to his rural audience from sketchy notes or less. Richard Baxter, in his mid-sixties, urged all would-be pastors to first apprentice themselves to veteran clergy in the countryside, from whom they could learn their trade, and where they could gain by practising clarity and force in spontaneous homiletic utterance. For urban pulpits, however, it seems that pastors and lecturers (preachers hired to supplement the non-preaching or poor preaching of the incumbent) continued to write full scripts of their sermons throughout the Puritan period, and it was their usual habit to preach series of sermons on a single text, passage, or theme – thus, in effect, to preach treatises, which, once preached, were well on the way to becoming books. In this way they were able to put much homiletical material into print in a relatively short time.

This is not, to be sure, the whole story. Puritan catechisms, and catechetical dialogues like Arthur Dent's *The Plain Man's*

Pathway to Heaven (1601; 40th ed., 1704), were written directly for the press. So were John Bunyan's imaginative products (most notably, *The Pilgrim's Progress, part 1*, 1678, *Part 2*, 1684; *The Holy War*, 1682; *The Life and Death of Mr Badman*, 1680), and probably indeed all the rest of his works. And scholarly pastors like John Owen and Richard Baxter wrote books in direct response to the books of others. Common to all the Puritan publications, however, was the consensus that whatever was produced, in whatever form and by whatever means, must be, not simply Bible-based in a formal way, but edifying to Christian readers, calculated to expand and deepen their knowledge of the Father, the Son, the Holy Spirit, and the divine way of grace, and it is this focus that gives Puritan pastoral writing its distinctive flavour.

The Puritans were, to a remarkable extent, a theologically homogeneous school of thought, and the simplest procedure for getting abreast of the beliefs that ruled their minds and warmed their hearts is to master the teaching of the Westminster Shorter Catechism, which the Church of Scotland's General Assembly in 1648 described as 'a Directory for catechizing such as are of weaker capacity,' meaning children and adults who for whatever reason needed to be treated as beginner Christians. Here, in 107 crisp questions and answers, with supporting Scriptures, the whole filling less than thirty pages in ordinary editions, is the quintessence of Puritan divinity. The definition of God; creation; providence; sin; the covenant of grace; the Lord Jesus Christ, our incarnate Redeemer, as our prophet, priest and king, first humiliated and then exalted; effectual calling into salvation, and the life of grace of those thus saved; the Decalogue, the basis of ethics; faith, repentance, and the sacraments; prayer, and specifically the Lord's Prayer – this is the ground that the Catechism covered, this was the structural form of Puritan soteriology, and this was the area of truth that was put under constant exploration by Puritanism's 'affectionate practical' authors. It was their belief that here is the essence of biblical teaching, to which all parts of the canon contribute; here is the heart of the gospel, to which both Testaments consistently point; here is where anyone reading the Bible with an open mind and heart will find themselves being led for self-assessment, self-condemnation, and self-giving to the risen, living Christ. The ground is in one sense familiar, for it is just mainstream Christianity, which all major versions of the faith embrace, with more or less accuracy, to be sure, when judged by Puritan standards. Believers who have read this paragraph thus far might perhaps be tempted to conclude that they are already abreast of what the Puritans have to offer, and so to leave them unread. But the Puritan way of occupying this central Christian ground has a quality that will uniquely enrich any reader, at any stage of their discipleship, and so may properly claim fullest attention from all.

The quality in question is analytical thoroughness. This stemmed from the Puritan understanding of the nature of Scripture on the one hand, and the condition of the members of their congregations on the other. Both these factors call for comment here.

Like Calvin and Reformation theologians as a body, the Puritans saw Scripture as consisting of two realities inseparably blended. One is human testimony, varied and diverse, to the human story of sin and grace in God's world, right from the beginning up to the life, death, rising and reigning of the Lord Jesus Christ. The other is God's own testimony, given in the very words of the human testimony by the Holy Spirit, to as much about His plans for, and providential management of, His world as He wants us, Christ's servants that we are, to know. The Puritan procedure for opening up this integrated, two-level biblical witness was spelled out by William Perkins in his *Art of Prophesying* (1595), a pioneer manual on the preaching ministry; it was thereafter prescribed in the *Westminster Directory for Public Worship* (1645), and practised in treatise after treatise throughout the Puritan period. The method was first to 'raise' – that is, extract – from the text doctrines – truths, that is, about God and humans in their mutual relations – then to explain them, and finally to apply them.

Here the characteristic Puritan passion for exhaustiveness would regularly kick in. Several doctrines would be raised from a single text. The explaining of each would involve relating it to other doctrines, and this could take up much time and / or space. Finally, the application would be branched out to cover different categories of readers (or, at first, listeners). A text, therefore, might well end up with a very large cartload of divinity attached to it.

Perkins's account of application distinguished seven sorts of listeners to sermons. First, some will be ignorant and unteachable; they must have their consciences pricked and stirred in an awakening way. Second, some will be ignorant but teachable; these need catechetically structured application, to show them how the doctrines relating to their salvation fit in to the overall framework of the faith. Third, some will be knowledgeable but uncommitted; their need is for the law, to humble them into repentance. Fourth, some will be aware of their sin and fearful of judgment; application for them must take them to the cross and saving mercy of Jesus Christ, according to the gospel. Fifth, some will be believers who need further grounding in how God's grace justifies, sanctifies and preserves His own. Sixth, some will be Christians who have fallen morally and are now in the grip of some particular sin; they need to hear of the grace that restores the penitent. Seventh, some are 'mixed' (mixed up? confused?); they need applications that will sort them out, as we say. All applications must be disciplined inferences from the doctrine being taught, and of course it is not possible to pursue all these lines of application in a single sermon. Yet something like half of an average Puritan sermon would be application, and the whole range of applications would be regularly covered in the course of an ordinary Puritan ministry. 'Discriminating' was the word that eventually emerged to characterise this applicatory method.

In the course of applying biblical doctrines to human hearts in these ways, Puritan preachers further displayed the analytical thoroughness that was, if we may put it so, their cultural style by their systematic procedure in searching those hearts. They sought to expose the complex of murky motivations and degenerate desires that Scripture and their own experience of the Christian life had shown them were there, forcing the subjects of sin's deceptions to face themselves and renounce the moral flaws and dishonesties that they found in themselves, masquerading as virtues or modes of wisdom. Using the doctrine or doctrines under consideration as a searchlight and scalpel, the preachers would detect ways in which sin thus prowls in our spiritual system and would then draw on the grace and lordship of Jesus Christ to induce sensitive self-assessment, radical repentance, and committed conflict henceforth against all these forms of evil. Puritanism was, among other things, a holiness movement, as we have noted already, and the preachers never lost sight of the fact that Christ calls to holiness those whom He saves. This emphasis on what Walter Marshall, one of them, called 'the gospel mystery of sanctification' gives the Puritan literary legacy a distinctive flavour and thrust throughout.

V

Basic to the Puritan mind-set, as is surely clear already, was a strong sense of the active presence of God, both in the world around, which is His creation ordered by His providence, and in each individual's personal life – one's own, to start with, and then that of everybody with whom one has to do. This pervasive sense of the awesome Creator's close-coming reality seems to have emerged in late fifteenth-century Western Europe, and it was certainly widespread in sixteenth and seventeenth century England. Factors feeding it there were the memory of the upheavals, including more than 300 Protestant martyrdoms, during the Reformation years from Henry VIII to Elizabeth; the spread of factual knowledge about God via high-quality Bible translations from Tyndale through the Geneva Bible to the King James version of 1611; the equally high-quality Biblicism of the Cranmerian Prayer Book, which was used Sunday by Sunday in all English churches; the dramatic life-and-death, villain-and-hero narratives of John Foxe's hugely influential

Acts and Monuments (later to become, slimmed down, his *Book of Martyrs*); and the impact of living under a constant threat from the armed forces of Roman Catholicism, currently warring for their faith on the European continent. Communal tension arising from these factors was a mark of English life all through the Puritan era, and the Puritans themselves seem to have felt it more acutely than most others. Also, for whatever reason, whether in connection with the foregoing items or not (nobody seems quite sure), the dramatic and expressive powers of the English language were being diligently mined by poets of distinction (Shakespeare, Marlowe, Spenser, Donne, Milton), and this linguistic colouring-up, if we may so describe it, undoubtedly contributed to an increased relational sensitivity and intensity in national life across the board; which in due course spilled over into the world of Puritan pastoral preaching and counselling. All Puritan communication was designed to confront people as clearly and inescapably as possible with the closeness of God – the God who searches us, and exposes us to ourselves; who both judges and loves, both condemns and justifies through His Son, Jesus Christ; who claims and commands us, while promising protection, preservation, and final reward; and who may not on any account be ignored.

The idiom of developed Puritan pulpitese, which is often labelled the 'plain' style, reflects what was happening to the language. Fanciful forms of expression and literary ornament for addressing the supposedly cultured had come into fashion towards the end of Elizabeth's reign, in the belief that thus adorned the Word would be weightier, and the preachers themselves would glorify God more. The masters of this stylistic splendour were Bishop Lancelot Andrewes and John Donne, Dean of St Paul's, London's cathedral. To the Puritans, however, such displays of preachers' cleverness only trivialised what they were saying. Puritan preachers themselves aimed at forceful utterance, but it was to be the forcefulness of someone banging at your door and shouting to you that your house was on fire. The classic expression of this urgency, all the more potent for being so personal, came from Richard Baxter, who in the preface to his *Treatise of Conversion* (1657) wrote as follows:

> The plainest words are the profitablest oratory in the weightiest matters ... it is hard for the necessitous reader to observe the matter of ornament and delicacy, and not to be carried away from the matter of necessity; and to hear or read a neat, concise, sententious discourse, and not be *hurt* by it; for it usually hindereth the due operation of the matter, keeps it from the heart, stops it in the fancy, and makes it seem as *light* as the style ... If we see a man fall into fire or water, we stand not upon *mannerliness* in plucking him out, but lay hands on him as we can without delay ... I shall never forget the relish of my soul, when God first warmed my heart with these matters, and when I was newly entered into a seriousness in religion; when I read such a book as Bishop Andrews' (*sic*) sermons, or heard such kind of preaching, I felt no life in it, methought they did but play with holy things ... But it was the plain and pressing downright preacher, that only seemed to me to be in good sadness [real earnest] ... and to speak with life, and light, and weight: and it was such kind of writings that were wonderfully pleasant and savoury to my soul. And I am apt to think that it is thus now with my hearers ... I must confess, that though I can better digest exactness and brevity, than I could so long ago, yet I as much value seriousness and plainness; and I feel in myself in reading or hearing, a despising of that wittiness as proud foolery ... As a stage-player, or morris-dancer, differs from a soldier or a king, so do those preachers from the true and faithful minister of Christ: and as they deal liker to players than preachers in the pulpit, so usually their hearers do rather come to play with a sermon, than to attend a message from the God of heaven about the life or death of their souls.

Here we behold the Puritan ideal of speaking for God as teacher, pastor, ambassador for Christ, spiritual physician, guide to life, herald of God, searcher of hearts, and persuader of truth. There must be no misunderstanding about this. Puritan rhetoric, though always didactic, was as far as possible from being unimaginative, drab and dull. It was brisk and energetic, pictorial and dramatic, within its orderliness often explosive, and always arresting and urgent; never somnolent, cool, casual or slapdash. Puritan sermons were meant to be remembered, meditated on, discussed and applied; that is why all the material was carefully arranged under headings, and why listeners were encouraged to take notes. The Puritan belief, as we have seen, was that it is supremely through preaching that God comes close, to deal and be dealt with regarding faith, repentance, conversion and the life of holiness. The preacher's expository and applicatory style needed to match the momentousness of this truly awesome agenda for the sermon situation, and to that end it needed to be as pointed, thrustful and memorable as possible. Preachers who rose to the occasion and were felt to bring God with them into the pulpit were called 'powerful,' and we should be thankful that much of their power can still be felt as, centuries later, we read their published work.

All of which leads us now to the second part of the present study.

Part 2:

Puritan Pastors in Profile

Puritan Pastors in Profile

Some years ago Christian Focus launched its Christian Heritage series of paperbacks, each containing a devotional gem from a member of the Puritan school of thought. I was asked to write an introduction to each, presenting the writer and his work and indicating something of its value for the present-day Christian reader. I accepted the assignment as a kind of challenge; the selections were not mine, but I applauded them, and found it enriching to compose essays that would celebrate the author, the book, and the benefit it brings in each case, and so tune readers in to what was before them and help them to get the best from it. These introductions are separately reprinted below, for their contents seem to me to admirably amplify and illustrate what the foregoing overview essay on Puritan pastors has sought to cover in general terms. They are, to be sure, somewhat forlorn when detached from the publications they prefaced; their full force, such as it is, will only, I think, be appreciated if one goes on to read what they introduced and then re-reads what I attempt to say about it; but they seem to be pieces that can stand alone if they have to, and that do in fact add substance to what I have said so far. The series is as follows:

1. Henry Scougal, *The Life of God in the Soul of Man.*
2. Stephen Charnock, *Christ Crucified.*
3. John Bunyan, *The Heavenly Footman.*
4. Matthew Henry, *The Pleasantness of a Religious Life.*
5. John Owen, *The Mortification of Sin.*
6. John Flavel, *Keeping the Heart.*
7. Thomas Boston, *The Art of Man-Fishing*, *The Crook in the Lot* and *Repentance.*

The Christian Heritage series remains in print for any who wish to invest in it.

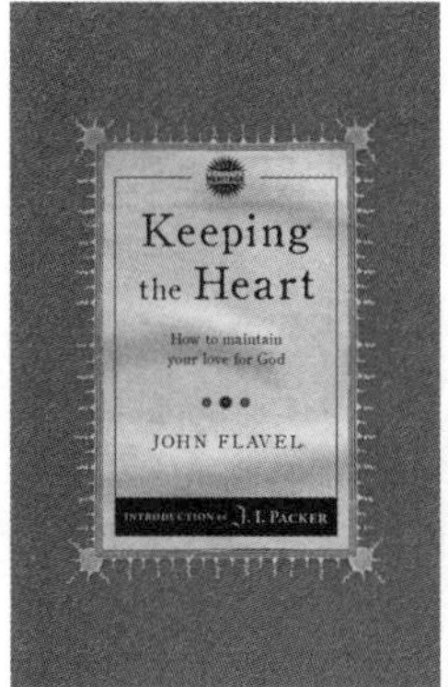
Keeping the Heart
How to maintain your love for God
JOHN FLAVEL
INTRODUCTION BY J. I. PACKER

The Life of God in the Soul of Man
Real Religion
HENRY SCOUGAL
INTRODUCTION BY J. I. PACKER

The Mortification of Sin
Dealing with sin in your life
JOHN OWEN
INTRODUCTION BY J. I. PACKER

The Pleasantness of a Religious Life
Life as good as it can be
MATTHEW HENRY
INTRODUCTION BY J. I. PACKER

Repentance
Turning from sin to God
THOMAS BOSTON
INTRODUCTION BY J. I. PACKER

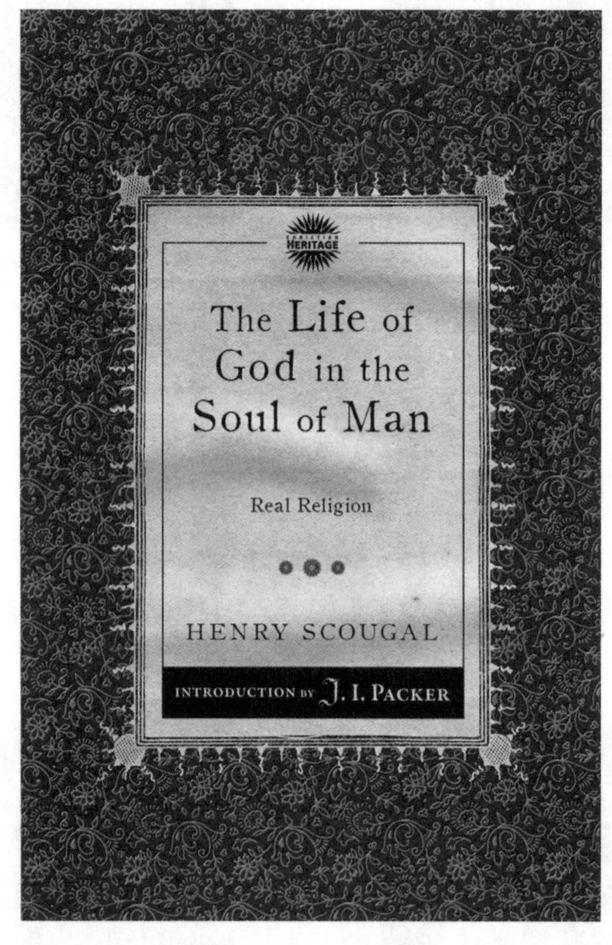

ISBN 978-1-78191-107-5

I

Henry Scougal

The Life of God in the Soul of Man

'I never knew what true religion was till God sent me this excellent treatise,' wrote George Whitefield.

When a man of Whitefield's stature applauds a book in such terms, it is our wisdom to sit up and take notice. For who was Whitefield? The 'Grand Itinerant', as his contemporaries called him, was, more than anyone else, the trail-blazing pioneer and personal embodiment of the eighteenth-century revival of vital Christianity in the West, the revival that shaped English-speaking society on both sides of the Atlantic for over a hundred years and that fathered the evangelical missionary movement which for the past two centuries has been taking the gospel literally round the world.

That epoch-making revival threw up many outstanding leaders, but head and shoulders above the rest were four giants, landmark figures not just for their own lifetime but for all later ages too: John Wesley, supreme as organiser, educator, pastoral leader, publicist and apologist; Charles Wesley, his younger brother, sublimest poet of Christian experience; Jonathan Edwards, America's greatest theologian; and with them, indeed in one sense ahead of them all, Whitefield, who for a generation till his death in 1770 was acknowledged as the focal figure of the entire movement. First to preach the transforming message of the new birth, first to take it into the open air and declare the world his parish, first to publish journals celebrating God's work in and through him, and first to set up societies for the nurturing of those who came to faith under his ministry. Whitefield proclaimed Christ tirelessly throughout Britain and colonial America, drawing huge crowds, winning thousands of souls, impacting myriads more, and gaining celebrity status of a kind matched only by Billy Graham and John Paul II in our time. Wesley's influence as a renewer of popular religion is sometimes credited with saving England from an upheaval like the French Revolution; if there is substance in such reasoning, Whitefield should receive greater credit, for his ministry ranged wider and his pulpit power was greater. We live at a time when uncertainty as to what constitutes true religion is more widespread, perhaps, than at any time since Christianity was born; we shall do well to recognise that the little old book that cleared Whitefield's mind on this basic matter might have something to say to us too.

Henry Scougal's exposition of 'true religion' (his phrase, echoed by Whitefield, meaning genuine Christianity) was from one standpoint the seed out of which the English side of the revival first sprouted; for the book was favourite reading in Oxford's Holy Club, where the Wesleys and Whitefield first came together. For half a century religious societies, as they were called, had been set up in various places to supplement the parish church's Sunday ministry by midweek gatherings for prayer, discussion, and the reading of works of devotion ('good books'). The society lampooned as the Holy Club was run by John Wesley in his capacity as an ordained priest and Fellow of Lincoln College. It was distinctive only for being in Oxford, where such a thing had not, it seems, been seen before, and for the ascetic intensity with which its dozen or so members pursued the goal of true religion. Whitefield, a tall, good-looking, well-spoken freshman from Gloucester, a servitor at Pembroke College – one, that is, who performed menial duties to finance his education – admired the Holy Club from afar, and wanted to join. Charles Wesley, himself a member, took a liking to Whitefield and gave him Scougal, which he eagerly devoured. An agonizing quest, evidently Scougal-sparked, for the life of God in his own soul then led to the dawning of an assured certainty that through the grace of Jesus Christ he was 'ransomed, healed, restored, forgiven' and truly born again.

I once heard a Christian testify, 'I knew I was converted when religion stopped being a duty and became a delight,' and that is something Whitefield could have said, for that was precisely what he felt. Once ordained, he preached the new birth as the door of entry into true religion as Scougal described it, and the English revival began. Without Scougal it might not have happened.

What precisely was it that Whitefield learned from Scougal? In a word, it was the inwardness and supernaturalness of biblical godliness. Not that Scougal's testimony here was in any way unique. During the century that followed the Reformation conflicts, English Puritans like Perkins, Owen and Baxter, Anglicans of the 'holy living' school like Jeremy Taylor, Lutheran pietists like Johannes Arndt, and Roman Catholic teachers like Ignatius Loyola, Francis de Sales, Teresa of Avila and John of the Cross, had all centred attention on the realities of the Christian's inner life, to such an extent that scholars can nowadays speak of the seventeenth-century devotional revival. In this study the Reformation debates about church, sacraments, justification and authority largely receded into the background; communion with the Father and the Son through the Spirit, lived out in the disciplined practice of patient love and humble obedience, was the common theme, and Scougal, a devoted soul himself, was able to draw on a rich legacy of fairly homogeneous thought about 'the life of God in the soul of man'. This helps to explain the extraordinary authority, maturity, and sureness of touch with which at the age of twenty-six he was able to analyse the reality of spiritual life. Granted, he was brilliant and precocious (he served as Professor of Philosophy in Aberdeen University for four years, from the age of nineteen); granted, he was the son of a minister, and a godly one, and had had every spiritual advantage in his upbringing plus, as it seems, a heart responsive to God from his earliest days; but even so, he could hardly have produced this little classic – for such it is – without the distilled wisdom of the seventeenth century behind him.

Scougal's life was short. Born in 1650, he was ordained in 1673 and served for a year in a country parish, a holy man excelling as preacher, catechist, and worship leader. In 1674 he was made Professor of Divinity at Aberdeen, where he diligently mentored ministerial students, impressing on them the gravity of the pastoral task, lending them books and helping them in many ways. A nineteenth-century reprint of Whitefield's sermons was discerningly titled *The Revived Puritan*; Scougal was another Anglican who qualified for that description. He died of tuberculosis in 1678.

'Christians,' declares Scougal, 'know by experience that true religion is a union of the soul with God, a real participation of the divine nature, the very image of God drawn upon the soul, or, in the apostle's phrase, "it is Christ formed within us".' It is 'life', the life of God within, in the sense of being spontaneous energy actively responding to the grace of God set forth in the gospel. Scougal calls it 'an inward, free and self-moving principle ... a new nature instructing and prompting'. Love, purity and humility are the three fundamental virtues in which this life takes form, and all three are blossomings of faith. 'Faith (is) ... a kind of sense, or feeling persuasion of spiritual things; it extends itself unto all divine truths; but in our lapsed estate, it hath a peculiar relation to the declarations of God's mercy and reconcilableness to sinners through a mediator; and therefore ... is ordinarily termed "faith in Jesus Christ".' The virtues themselves are to be conceived in a way that sees acts as the outworking of attitudes and attitudes as the expression of motives; so Scougal defines them as follows.

Love, basically, is love of God: 'a delightful and affectionate sense of the divine perfections, which makes the soul resign and sacrifice itself wholly unto him, desiring above all things to please him, and delighting in nothing so much as in fellowship and communion with him, and being ready to do or suffer anything for his sake, or at his pleasure ... A soul thus possessed with divine love must needs be enlarged towards all mankind ... this is ... charity ... under which all parts of justice, all the duties we owe to our neighbour, are eminently comprehended; for he who doth truly love all the world ... so far from wronging or injuring any person ... will resent any evil that befalls others, as if it happened to himself.'

Purity is 'a due abstractedness from the body and mastery over the inferior appetites ... such a temper and disposition of mind as makes a man despise and abstain from all pleasures and delights of sense or fancy which are sinful in themselves, or tend to ... lessen our relish of more divine and intellectual (he means, God-centred and rational) pleasures, which doth also infer a resoluteness to undergo all those hardships he may meet with in the performance of his duty: so that not only chastity and temperance, but also Christian courage and magnanimity may come under this head.'

And humility means 'a deep sense of our own meanness, with a hearty and affectionate acknowledgment of our owing all that we are to the divine bounty; which is always accompanied with a profound submission to the will of God, and great deadness to the glory of the world, and the applause of men.'

'These qualities,' says Scougal, 'are the very foundation of heaven laid in the soul,' just as they are the basic elements of genuine Christlikeness here and now. The rest of his book is a celebration of these qualities, with encouragement to develop habits of repentance and discipline in using the means of grace (thought, prayer, and the Lord's Supper) so as to engender all three ever more radically and robustly in one's personal life.

Scougal never loses sight of the inwardness of true religion, as a state of being that starts in our hearts, nor of the fact that it is a supernatural product, 'having God for its author, and being wrought in the souls of men by the power of the Holy Spirit'; so we do not find him slipping into the self-reliant, performance-oriented, surface-level, ego-focussed, living-by-numbers type of instruction that is all too common among Christians today. He knows that personal change will not occur without use of means, just as he knows that no use of means will change the heart without God's blessing, and he marks out the path of change with admirable balance.

One could wish, however, that his exposition had been more explicitly and emphatically Christ-centred. Like so many seventeenth-century writers, he lets himself assume that his readers know all about Jesus and need only to be told about real religion, the life of faith and faith-full turning Godward as opposed to the orthodoxism, formalism, emotionalism and legalism that masquerade as Christianity while being in truth a denial of it. Had Scougal elaborated on the Christian's union with Christ, which the New Testament sees as regeneration by the Holy Spirit; had he explained incorporation into the Saviour's risen life, whereby Jesus's motivating passion to know and love and serve and please and honour and glorify the Father is implanted in sinners so that it is henceforth their own deepest desire too; had he thus shown, in black and white, that imitating Jesus's aims and attitudes in serving God and mankind is for the born-again the most natural, indeed the only natural, way of living, while for the unregenerate it is hard to the point of impossible; his little treatise would have been immeasurably stronger. As it is, Scougal's profile of divine life in human souls is much more complete than his answer to the question, how do I get into it? – or, how does it get into me? This is a limitation.

To be sure, there are real strengths in Scougal's account of the means of grace for the changing of the heart, particularly when he directs us to meditation – sustained thought, that is – on the 'vanity and emptiness of worldly enjoyments', the truth of Christianity, and the redeeming love of God as shown in the saving ministry of our Lord Jesus Christ. He is strong too when he urges us to form habits of behaving as if our hearts were changed even though as yet they are not. This is more than 'fake it till you make it'; Scougal is telling us to give God proof that we are serious and sincere in seeking inward renewal, for he knows that evidence of sincerity is something God regularly requires as a condition of answering our prayers. With these emphases, however, should be linked specific directions on looking to and coming to the living Christ Himself, believing on Him, trusting in Him, and waiting for Him till we know that we are His and He is ours – the sort of directions that Whitefield himself was later to give during the last half-hour of many thousands of evangelistic messages. Scougal's omission here, which leaves the impression that godliness blossoms in us as a kind of natural growth, is certainly a shortcoming.

It will be appropriate as we close to cite more fully Whitefield's witness to what Scougal gave him. This comes from a sermon preached in the last year of his life, taken down as he spoke and not corrected.

> When I was sixteen years of age, I began to fast twice a week for thirty-six hours together, prayed many times a day, received the sacrament every Lord's day, fasting myself almost to death all the forty days of Lent, during which I made it a point of duty never to go less than three times a day to public worship, besides seven times a day to my private prayers, yet I knew no more that I was to be born again in God, born a new creature in Christ Jesus, than if I were never born at all ...
>
> I must bear testimony to my old friend Mr Charles Wesley; he put a book into my hands, called *The Life of God in the Soul of Man*, whereby God showed me, that I must be born again, or be damned.

> I know the place: it may be superstitious, perhaps, but whenever I go to Oxford, I cannot help running to that place where Jesus Christ first revealed himself to me, and gave me the new birth ... How did my heart rise, how did my heart shudder, like a poor man that is afraid to look into his account-books, lest he should find himself a bankrupt; yet shall I burn that book, shall I throw it down, shall I put it by, or shall I search into it? I did, and holding the book in my hand, thus addressed the God of heaven and earth: Lord, if I am not a Christian, if I am not a real one, God, for Jesus Christ's sake, show me what Christianity is, that I may not be damned at last. I read a little further ... O, says the author, they that know anything of religion, know it is a vital union with the Son of God, Christ formed in the heart; O what a ray of divine life did then break in upon my poor soul ... from that moment God has been carrying on his blessed work in my soul: and as I am now fifty-five years of age ... I tell you, my brethren ... I am more and more convinced that this is the truth of God, and without it you never can be saved by Jesus Christ ...

Thus God used Scougal to awaken the man who himself came later to be known as the Awakener. And all that remains to be said is that some today, who would call themselves Christians if asked, clearly stand in need of a similar awakening: which Scougal, under God, may bring them, if only they will read his smooth late-seventeenth-century rhetoric thoughtfully and let it speak to them. Real Christians will gain from Scougal a healthy reminder that heart-change and character-change thence resulting is what their faith is all about, and the self-deceived will be forced to face the fact that those who have not yet been so changed are not yet Christians at all. Scougal's word to them will thus have been preparation for the humble hearing of the gospel invitation, which many today would otherwise fail to hear because they are unaware that they need to hear it, and which Whitefield, near the time when he uttered the testimony quoted above, verbalised as follows:

> Sinners in Zion, baptised heathens, professors but not possessors, formalists, believing unbelievers, talking of Christ, talking

of grace, orthodox in your creeds, but heterodox in your lives, turn ye, turn ye, Lord help you to turn to him, turn ye to Jesus Christ, and may God turn you inside out ... may that glorious Father that raised Christ from the dead, raise your dead souls! ... Bless the Lord that Jesus stands with pitying eyes, and outstretched arms, to receive you now. Will you go with the man? Will you accept of Christ? Will you begin to live now? May God say, Amen; may God pass by, not in anger, but in love ... and say to you dead sinners, come forth, live a life of faith on earth, live a life of vision in heaven; even so, Lord Jesus: *Amen*.

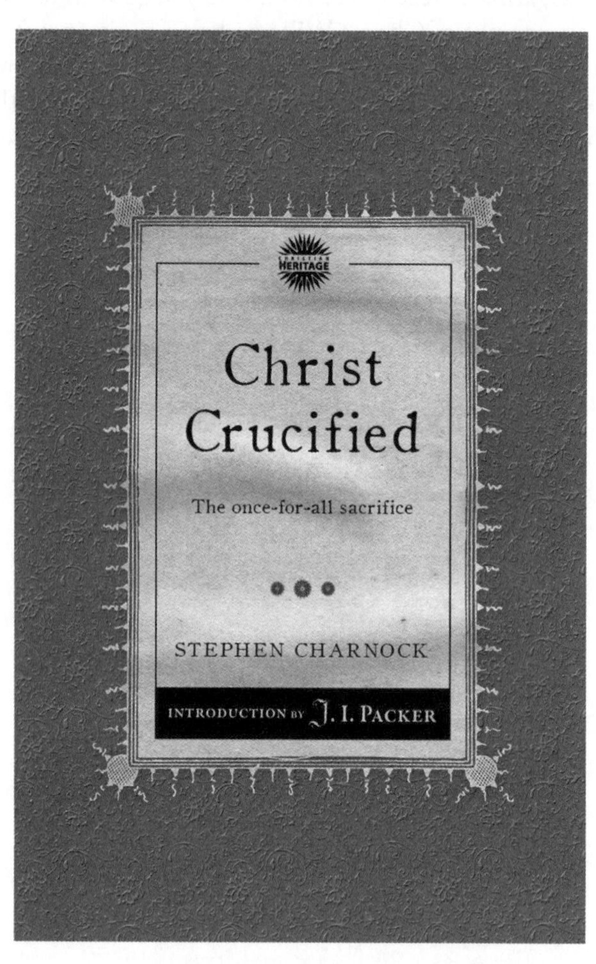

ISBN 978-1-84550-976-7

2

Stephen Charnock

Christ Crucified

The central fact in Christianity is the reality, historical, eternal and inescapable, of Jesus Christ, who is the Son of God in the trinitarian sense of being God the Son, who is the future Judge of all human beings everywhere, and whom the gospel proclaims as Saviour, Redeemer and Friend to all who become His followers. Let us be clear that where Jesus is not acknowledged as God incarnate, crucified, risen, reigning and returning, there is no Christianity, whatever liberals in and outside the churches may say to the contrary.

Again, the central focus in Christianity is the knowledge, conceptual and relational, objective and personal, of Christ crucified. This is a knowledge that involves both the head and the heart, and that begets a new loyalty, a new love and a new life. It is the theme with which the Puritan Stephen Charnock is dealing in the work that I am here introducing. Let us be clear that apart from this knowledge there are no Christians, and it is mere confusion not to recognise this.

Charnock, ministering in nominally Christian Britain three centuries ago, could count on general assent to the positions I have just stated. But that is something no Christian communicator today dare do. The man in the street, as we like to say (and the woman in the street, as feminists would like us to say) sees Christianity as a moral code rather than as good news of salvation, and Jesus as a dead teacher rather than a living Saviour, and spiritual life as New Age-type meditation for self-improvement, and religious commitment as a hobby for those who care about that sort of thing. That we all live in God's presence and under His eye, and that we must one day answer to Him for the lives we have lived, and that our humanity is so out of shape through sin that we need a Saviour as urgently as persons with brain tumours need a surgeon, are truths that never enter most people's minds. In this climate of opinion it is no wonder if Christians themselves become unclear and uncertain about central elements in their own faith. If we do, however, that is all the more reason why we should listen to Charnock, who of all the Puritans is the most brisk and businesslike when it comes to saying things straight.

Charnock assumes that those he addresses are interested in his themes, and so are willing to concentrate on his unfolding of them. In his day many were: 'able ministers' (so his first editors tell us) 'loved to sit at his feet, for they received by one sermon of his those instructions which they could not get by many books or sermons of others'.[1] Popular communication today, however, rarely confronts us with anything so concentrated as a paragraph of Charnock, and unless his readers are seriously concerned they will flag. Perhaps I can do something to generate or reinforce a concern in the hearts of you who read this that will ensure that you don't flag when you get to Charnock – let us see. I may fail, I know – but it will not be for want of trying! First, however, a further word about Charnock himself.

Stephen Charnock, 1628–1680

Born in London, and born again at Cambridge University some time in the 1640s, Charnock was seen as a coming man, and was sent to Dublin as chaplain to Oliver Cromwell's son Henry, governor of Ireland, in 1655. There he gained a great reputation

1 *Works of Stephen Charnock* (Edinburgh: James Nichol, 1864), I.xxiv.

as a preacher. The Restoration, however, ended his Irish ministry, and he had no stated charge thereafter till he was called to share with Thomas Watson the pastorate of an elite nonconforming congregation that met in London at Crosby Hall. That lasted five years, from 1675 to his death in 1680. A passionately studious man, apparently a bachelor, he ordinarily put in five twelve-hour days per week in his study, and wrote out everything he proposed to say in public. It seems that he conceived the idea of preaching a complete systematico-practical theology (as we needs must call it) at Crosby Hall, and that his massive unfinished Discourses on the Existence and Attributes of God (over 600,000 words and 1,000 pages of smallish print in the 1864 edition of his collected works) were the start of it. (He died, we are told, while 'looking what to say next of the mercy, grace, and goodness of God'. [2]) These Discourses are giant-size Puritan sermons, each built on a text and laid out with doctrine, reason (exposition and defence), and use (application) in the standard Puritan manner, and each of them, given in full, would have occupied several hour-long preachments. Perhaps Charnock actually delivered them this way; and perhaps this, plus the fact that at Crosby Hall his failing memory and eyesight obliged him to read his sermon scripts through a magnifying glass, word for word, instead of speaking extempore without notes as in Dublin, helps to explain why many, even in that theological age, found him both heavy and over their heads, despite the easy handling of ideas that is one of his chief strengths. His smaller-scale treatment of Christ's death, however, flows very simply and will not baffle today's attentive reader in any way.

The Cross of Christ

I said at the outset that where the Lord Jesus is not confessed as God incarnate, crucified, risen, reigning and returning, and where there is no focus on the personal knowledge of Christ crucified, there is no Christianity. When I said that, bold as it

2 ibid., I.xxv.

sounds, I was defining Christianity in New Testament terms. For in the New Testament the cross of Christ is highlighted as, so to speak, the hinge and fulcrum of the gospel, the event that opened for us sinners a path to peace with God, power from God, and a prospect of glory through God that exceeds our wildest dreams. The gospels, as is often noted, are precisely passion stories with detailed introductions, telling us what led to the crucifixion so that we understand it when it comes. The vivid detail and calculated poignancy with which Matthew, Mark, Luke, and John, four skilful authors, tell the story of the cross exceed in intensity all that precedes, and the resurrection reports that follow, and thus identify the passion of Jesus as the true climax of each gospel. The theme of the book of Revelation is the twofold triumph of the crucified Lord, the slain Lamb, namely that which was at His first coming when He shed His blood for us and that which will be at His second coming when all is made new. And in the epistles, which are sermons about discipleship in letter form, the cross is central and basic to all the formative teaching that is given with regard to both faith (that is to say, belief and trust) and conduct (that is to say, motivation and action).

To be specific. The cross is the burden of the apostolic gospel ('we preach Christ crucified', 1 Cor. 1:23; cf. 1:18; 2:2). It is the centrepiece of God's eternal plan of grace ('you were redeemed ... with the precious blood of Christ, a lamb ... chosen before the creation ... revealed in these last times for your sake,' 1 Pet. 1:18-20; cf. John. 3:16 f.; 10:14-18; Gal. 4:4 f.). It is a sacrifice for sins ('Christ died for our sins according to the Scriptures,' 1 Cor. 15:3), quenching the divine wrath against sinners ('making peace through his blood, shed on the cross', Col. 1:20; cf. Eph. 2:18-20), securing our present justification and adoption and guaranteeing our future hope as God's heirs ('Since we have now been justified by his blood, how much more shall we be saved from God's wrath through him!', Rom. 5:9; 'He who did not spare his own Son, but gave him up for us all – how will he not also, along with him, graciously give us all things?'

Rom. 8:32). It is the mediatorial initiative (for Christ's passion was truly His action) that established Him in His saving role, as the author of salvation and so the proper object of saving faith ('The life I live ... I live by faith in the Son of God, who loved me and gave himself for me', Gal. 2:20; 'through faith in his blood', Rom. 3:25). It is the reality signified by the two sacramental ordinances that Jesus imposed ('baptised into his death ... buried with him through baptism into death', Rom. 6:3, 4; 'This is my body, which is for you' ... 'This cup is the new covenant in my blood; do this, whenever you drink it, in remembrance of me', 1 Cor. 11:24-25). It sets us standards of self-giving love and self-denying humility ('live a life of love, just as Christ loved us and gave himself up for us', Eph. 5:2; 'Jesus Christ laid down his life for us. And we ought to lay down our lives for our brothers', 1 John 3:16; 'he humbled himself and became obedient to death – even death on a cross', Phil. 2:8). It calls for, and calls forth, consecrated service and devotion ('You are not your own; you were bought at a price. Therefore honour God with your body', 1 Cor. 6:19, 20; 'Christ's love compels us ... one died for all ... that those who live should no longer live for themselves, but for him who died for them', 2 Cor. 5:14, 15). It models endurance in the face of hostility and pain ('Christ suffered for you, leaving you an example, that you should follow in his steps', 1 Pet. 2:21; cf. Heb. 12:2 f.).

So we might go on, but surely the point is clear enough by now. Trusting, loving and following Jesus necessitates keeping the cross in view at all times. Our living Lord calls for what we may call cruciform discipleship, clear-headed, open-eyed and whole-hearted. 'May I never boast except in the cross of our Lord Jesus Christ, through which the world has been crucified to me, and I to the world' (Gal. 6:14). The cross must shape our faith, and thereby reshape our entire lives.

Celebrating Christ Crucified

Charnock's expositions, though clear and deep, sometimes seem cool and dry. This is because his style is intensely analytical, and his mind moves fast and verbalises itself economically, as if he were writing notes for an exposition rather than composing the exposition itself. His power of boiling down and compressing excites admiration, but can leave the wisdom and truth he sets forth still at a distance from our inner being. As his portrait depicts him as having bony features,[3] so his writing reveals him as a man of bony thoughts who sees it as our part rather than his to put flesh on the bones and warm up the thoughts so that they gain heart-piercing power. The Puritan ideal was to be a 'practical affectionate divine', meaning one who cleared heads, strengthened hearts, and settled consciences with equal skill; Charnock is as strong as any in clearing heads, but is less able than some to stir the imagination and touch the heart. It must have been this distancing of himself as a communicator from the affectional side of life that led some to complain that his sermons had in them only 'morality or metaphysics'[4] – for they contain, not too little evangelical doctrine, but, if anything, too much, packed too tight. Evidently he thought that the dramatising and interiorising of gospel truth was for his hearers to do by personal meditation, rather than for him to attempt by pulpit rhetoric.

Here, he deals with the theme of Christ crucified by dwelling successively on the sovereignty, love and justice of the Father who ordained the cross, the dignity, willingness and agony of the Son in enduring it, the transformed relationship with God that flows from it, and the gratitude, delight, and enlarging of repentance, faith, boldness in approaching God, holiness as a life-goal, and 'comfort' (encouragement) as a life-support, that knowledge of Christ crucified should engender in us. The Reformed and Puritan understanding of penal substitution at Calvary is expressed with plain and simple precision. But it is a cool, bony treatment, which it is left to us to warm up for ourselves. How shall we do that? I offer the following suggestion.

3 ibid., I.xxiv.

4 ibid., I.xxiii.

Before you start to read Charnock, spend time with the following three lyrics, each of which embodies some knowledge of Christ crucified in meditations that touch the depths of the Christian heart. Let them search you, and move you, as they are well calculated to do.[5] The first is by the latter-day Puritan, Isaac Watts. It is well known.

When I survey the wondrous cross,
On which the Prince of Glory died,
My richest gain I count but loss,
And pour contempt on all my pride.

Forbid it, Lord, that I should boast
Save in the death of Christ my God:
All the vain things that charm me most,
I sacrifice them to his blood.

See from his head, his hands, his feet,
Sorrow and love flow mingled down;
Did e'er such love and sorrow meet,
Or thorns compose so rich a crown?

Were the whole realm of nature mine,
That were an offering far too small;
Love so amazing, so divine,
Demands my soul, my life, my all.

The second is also by Isaac Watts. It is less familiar, and more heart-wrenching.

Alas! and did my Saviour bleed
And did my Sovereign die?
Would he devote that sacred head
For such a worm as I?

Was it for crimes that I had done
He groaned upon the tree?
Amazing pity! grace unknown!
And love beyond degree!

---

5 Quoted from Christian Hymns (Bridgend: Evangelical Movement of Wales, second ed., 1985), nos. 203, 197, 540.

Well might the sun in darkness hide,
And shut his glories in,
When God, the mighty Maker, died
For man, the creature's sin.

Thus might I hide my blushing face
While his dear cross appears;
Dissolve my heart in thankfulness,
And melt my eyes to tears.

But drops of grief can ne'er repay
The debt of love I owe:
Here, Lord, I give myself away;
'Tis all that I can do.

The third is by Augustus Toplady, an eighteenth-century evangelical, author of 'Rock of Ages'. It is not at all well known in the modern Christian world. It deals with the self-doubt and inner dread that all regenerate persons face sooner or later.

From whence this fear and unbelief?
Hath not the Father put to grief
His spotless Son for me?
And will the righteous Judge of men
Condemn me for that debt of sin
Which, Lord, was charged on thee?

Complete atonement thou hast made,
And to the utmost thou hast paid
Whate'er thy people owed;
How then can wrath on me take place,
If sheltered in thy righteousness,
And sprinkled with thy blood?

If thou hast my discharge procured
And freely in my room endured
The whole of wrath divine,
Payment God cannot twice demand,
First at my bleeding Surety's hand
And then again at mine.

Turn then, my soul, unto thy rest!
The sorrows of thy great High Priest
Have bought thy liberty;
Trust in his efficacious blood,
Nor fear thy banishment from God,
Since Jesus died for thee.

Now, with the preciousness of the cross to you firmly fixed in your mind and heart through meditating on these lyrics, read Charnock, looking for the full-scale theology that underlies, and justifies, the low thoughts of yourself, and the high thoughts of God the Father and God the Son, with which your broodings have left you. I think you will find that sentence after sentence in Charnock's ordered march lights up and glows in your heart, as illuminating and undergirding things you are feeling. End by working through the lyrics again, elaborating to yourself in God's presence what they say about what has specially struck you in Charnock's presentation. This is only a suggestion, and you are free to ignore it. But please don't accuse Charnock of being dry till you've tried it! That's all I ask.

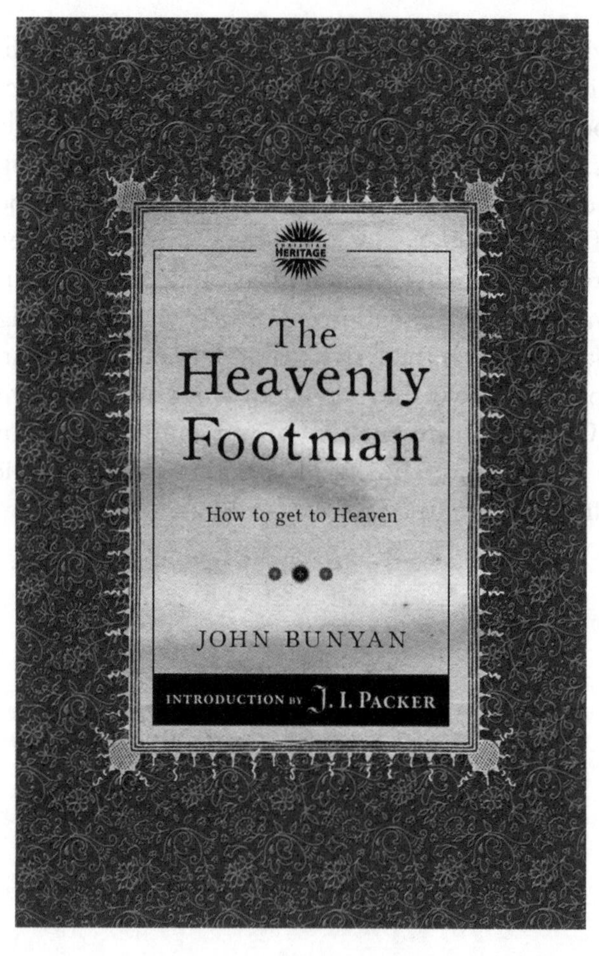

ISBN 978-1-84550-650-6

3

John Bunyan

The Heavenly Footman

In the pre-photography world of the seventeenth century, persons of quality by birth and persons of distinction for their achievements were regularly painted, drawn, or engraved by professional artists. Artists, willy-nilly, being the imaginative people they are, interpret their subjects differently, picturing what they think they see as they look at them, so that portraits of the same person may vary in striking ways. So it is with the two surviving likenesses of Bunyan. That by Thomas Sadler, which hangs in London's National Portrait Gallery, shows him as he was in 1685, at the age of fifty-six. He is dressed for the pulpit, has a Bible in his hand, and looks very serious, purposeful and under tension; indeed, he is almost scowling. You feel this is Bunyan the Lord's messenger, looking at you in preparation for preaching to you in an applicatory and admonitory way. But there is also a pencil study of Bunyan from the same period by Robert White, who we are told had a flair for sympathetic portraiture. White's Bunyan, like Sadler's, looks at us, but in quite a different way: he is relaxed, genial, faintly smiling yet somewhat withdrawn, a man (you would say) with a great deal of inner life, at peace in himself, and ready to share what he sees and knows.

Both date from the days when *Pilgrim's Progress* had catapulted its author into stardom. Maybe White made Bunyan too handsome while Sadler made him too rugged; yet there is truth in both ways of seeing him. His homiletic writings really are tense and fierce, and no doubt his preaching was the same; while *Pilgrim's Progress*, and other writings in the same allegorical and parabolic vein, reveal whimsy and wit, and are sometimes downright comic. These are the two sides of John Bunyan, a faithful minister and a fascinating man.

By birth he was not a person of quality; just the reverse. He was the son of a brazier whose family had come down in the world and who now ran a metalworker's shop in Elstow, a village of sixty-nine cottages outside the town of Bedford. He was sent to school to learn to read and write, but was soon withdrawn so that he could learn his father's trade. No doubt the plan was that he should work in the shop permanently. In 1644, however, when he was sixteen, his mother and sister died, his father remarried, and he himself was drafted for a two-and-a-half year stint in the Parliamentary army. It is not perhaps surprising that when he got back to Elstow, a 'veteran' (as today's Americans would say) still in his teens, rather than settle down in the shop he struck out for independence; he became a tinker (that is, a metalworking itinerant), launched himself into poverty by marriage, and so continued till he was jailed in 1660. Tinkers, being itinerants and thus potential getaway artists, were thought of as rascals, like shepherds in Jesus's day and tramps in ours, and the tinkering trade was not one that would make a man rich. It was hardly an auspicious beginning to Bunyan's career.

But by the end of his life he was a celebrity. He was an established Christian writer, whose *Pilgrim's Progress* was a runaway best-seller; he was a popular preacher, who drew crowds of thousands in London and of hundreds when he preached in Bedford, where he now pastored a church, and in the villages around; he was a friend of the great John Owen, who told Charles II that he would gladly give all his learning to be able to preach with Bunyan's power; he was called 'Bishop Bunyan' behind his back; and he sat for two of the top artists of his day. He had, as we would say, arrived.

The story of the progress of this pilgrim divides neatly into three periods, thus:

(1) The years 1648–60 were Bunyan's time of discovery. First, over a five-year period of soul-shaking ups and downs, which he later chronicled for the encouraging of his own converts in *Grace Abounding to the Chief of Sinners*, he found peace with God. His spiritual quest began when he married a godly man's daughter whose dowry consisted of two Puritan works, Arthur Dent's *Plain Man's Pathway to Heaven* and Lewis Bayley's *Practice of Piety*. He started attending church; stopped swearing, dancing and acting up; read the Bible; met some poor born-again women from a new church in Bedford and came to know John Gifford, their pastor; became Christ-centred and cross-centred through reading Luther on Galatians; spent two years fearing he had committed the unpardonable sin of abandoning Christ; and finally, in 1653, was baptised by Gifford in the river Ouse as a credible convert.

Then, second, he found he had a gift for pulpit ministry. Having gone as a trainee with members of the Bedford church who preached in the villages, and having testified and exhorted in small groups, Bunyan was formally instated as a lay preacher in 1656, and from then on fulfilled his own village ministry with much acceptance. His emphasis was constantly evangelistic: 'I found my spirit leaned most after awakening and converting work.'

Third, he found he had a gift for writing popular Christian literature. He began with polemics: *Some Gospel Truths Opened*

(1656) and *A Vindication of ... Some Gospel-Truths Opened* (1657) were against Quakerism. *A Few Sighs from Hell* (1658) and *The Doctrine of the Law and Grace Unfolded* (1659) came next. Articulate and a fast worker, with remarkable natural powers of analysis and argument, Bunyan never looked back from this beginning; he wrote and wrote, and by the end of his life had produced sixty treatises of different sizes, amounting in all to something like two million words.

(2) The years 1660–72 were Bunyan's time of dishonour, when for nonconformity he was confined to Bedford jail. The local magistrates, anxious to establish their identity as servants of the newly restored monarchy and about-to-be-restored Church of England, thought it good to make an example of Bedfordshire's most popular preacher, indicting and imprisoning him as a subversive who would not promise to not preach at non-Anglican assemblies. In prison Bunyan had no heating and slept on straw, but he enjoyed fair health, kept cheerful and wrote books. Also, to support his wife and children, he made 'many hundred grosse of long-tagged thread laces' which were then sold. Widely acknowledged as a man of spiritual authority, he counselled visitors, preached to the inmates regularly, and was sometimes let out to preach as well. Charles II's Declaration of Indulgence brought about his release in 1672. The church had formally appointed him pastor just before that, and pastoral ministry was his role for the rest of his life.

(3) The years 1672–88 were Bunyan's years of distinction, both as a preacher and as an author. *Pilgrim's Progress*, begun it seems during a further six month-spell in prison in 1675, was published in 1678, and sold like hot cakes. *The Life and Death of Mr Badman* (1680), *The Holy War* (1682), and part two of *Pilgrim's Progress* (1684), confirmed Bunyan's standing as a writer not simply of devotional treatises in the well-known

homiletic manner of a hundred Puritans before him, but of wonderfully vivid, racy, didactic-parabolic-allegorical stories which one way and another anchored evangelical faith in the world of common-man life. Altogether sixty books of different sorts came from Bunyan's pen during the thirty years of his writing career, and they are all worth reading still.

Something more must be said here about *Pilgrim's Progress*, which is both the best of Bunyan and a perfect pictorial index to the Puritan understanding of the Christian life. Secular study sees it as the start of the English novel, by reason of its quest-plot and its interplay of character, but Bunyan himself viewed it as a teaching tool – a didactic parable explaining the path of piety to ordinary people; a series of enlightening similitudes (Bunyan's word) about godliness and its opposite; a biblical dream tale with characters drawn from waking life to illustrate spiritual realities; a story that by God's grace might become the reader's own story as he or she went along. In the versified Apology that introduces part one, Bunyan tells us how it all started.

> When at the first I took my Pen in hand
> Thus for to write, I did not understand
> That I at all should make a little Book
> In such a mode; Nay, I had undertook
> To make another, which when almost done
> Before I was aware, I this begun.
> And thus it was: I writing of the Way
> and Race of Saints, in this our Gospel-Day,
> Fell suddenly into an Allegory
> About their Journey, and the way to Glory,
> In more than twenty things, which I set down;
> This done, I twenty more had in my Crown,
> And they again began to multiply,
> Like sparks that from the coals of fire do fly ...
> Thus I set Pen to Paper with delight,
> And quickly had my thoughts in black and white,

For having now my Method by the end,
Still as I pull'd, it came; and so I penn'd
It down; until at last it came to be
For length and breadth the bigness which you see ...
This Book it chalketh out before thine eyes
The man that seeks the everlasting Prize:
It shows you whence he comes, whither he goes,
What he leaves undone, also what he does;
It also shows you how he runs and runs
Till he unto the Gate of Glory comes ...
This book will make a Traveller of thee
If by its Counsel thou wilt ruled be;
It will direct thee to the Holy Land
If thou wilt its Directions understand ...
Would'st read thyself, and read thou know'st not what
And yet know whether thou art blest or not
By reading the same lines? O then come hither
And lay my Book, thy Head, and Heart together.

'The man that seeks the everlasting Prize ... runs and runs,' says Bunyan. Though the pilgrim in his story walks most of the way, he starts by running, once Evangelist has given him his first directions, and Bunyan makes a point of it: 'So I saw in my Dream, that the Man began to run ... the Man put his fingers in his ears, and ran on crying, Life! Life! Eternal Life!' Running, for Bunyan, is a picture of wholehearted effort to get away from something dreadful and get to something wonderful; in that sense, the pilgrim runs constantly, even when the story shows him walking and talking, as most of the time it does. This brings us to *The Heavenly Footman*. 'Footman' here means, not flunkey or foot-soldier, but a traveller on foot ('Such footmen as thee and I are,' as Christian says to Hopeful); 'heavenly' means heading for heaven as the goal; and the piece itself is a written-up sermon on 1 Corinthians 9:24 of which the burden is, quite simply – run!

When Bunyan wrote it is not certain, for it was not published in his lifetime: his friend Charles Doe brought it out in 1692, four years after his death. But the thoughts that *The Footman* develops are so much an echo of *Pilgrim's Progress* that it is hard to doubt that the sermon was written very soon after Bunyan finished the allegory. George Offer, Bunyan's mid-nineteenth century editor, draws this out:

> Is there a Slough of Despond to be passed, and a hill Difficulty to be overcome? Here the footman is reminded of 'many a dirty step, many a high hill, a long and tedious journey through a vast howling wilderness;' but he is encouraged, 'the land of promise is at the end of the way.' Must the man that would win eternal glory draw his sword, put on his helmet, and fight his way into the temple – the heavenly footman must press, crowd, and thrust through all that stands between heaven and his soul. Did Ignorance, who perished from the way, say to the pilgrims, 'You go so fast, I must stay awhile behind?' He who runs to heaven is told that the heavy-heeled, lazy, wanton, and foolish professor will not attain the prize. The wicket-gate at the head of the way, is all-important; none can get to heaven unless they enter by Christ, the door and the way, so the footman is reminded that it matters not how fast he runs, he can never attain the prize, if he is in the wrong road. Did the pilgrims so severely suffer from entering upon Byepath-meadow (*sic*), and even after that bitter experience were they again misled into a bye path, by a black man clothed in white raiment? Our footman is warned – Beware then of bye and crooked paths that lead to death and damnation ... Did the poor pilgrims go grunting, puffing, and sighing, one tumbleth over a bush, another sticks fast in the dirt, one cries out, I am down, and another, Ho! where are you? So the footman is told that he will 'meet with cross, pain, and wearisomeness to the flesh, with briars and quagmires, and other encumbrances,' through all of which he must persevere. Did Formalist and Hypocrite turn off

> into bye-ways at the foot of the hill Difficulty, and miserably perish? Did Mistrust and Timorous run back for fear of the persecuting lions, Church and State? So the man that runs for heaven is cautioned – 'Some when they come at the cross can go no further, but back again to their sins they go, stumble and break their necks, or turn aside to the left or to the right, and perish. Be not ready to halt, nor run hobbling ...' Or, as Paul puts it in the text which this sermon opens up, 'So run, that ye may obtain.'

The Heavenly Footman, first to last, is a single sustained exhortation to run, to run hard, and to keep running, along the path of life. Bunyan assumes that his readers already know the objective truths of the gospel that *Pilgrim's Progress* pictures for them, and now concentrates on raising consciousness and generating commitment with regard to gaining heaven and escaping hell. Here, as in other of his homiletical writings, Bunyan's intensity almost overwhelms you. His sense of hell's horrors, and of the truth of God's threatenings to the careless and insincere that match His promises to the faithful, is tremendously strong, and he commands a flow of words that makes him more able than most to make us feel what he feels himself. It is truly 'awakening and converting work' that he is engaged in here. Having formulated the teaching of his text as *they that will have heaven must run for it*, he rings the changes of why and how to run, and deploys motivating thoughts that should set you and keep you running, and jolt you out of any complacent apathy, or laziness, or as he calls it slothfulness, that may have settled down on your spirit. Perhaps the most piercing of all his remarks about this are contained in 'An Epistle to All the Slothful and Careless People' which he prints as a foreword, but which he undoubtedly wrote after completing the book, while the thoughts he had deployed were still boiling in his mind. Feel the force of these extracts from it:

> This I dare to be bold to say, no greater shame can befall a man, than to see that he hath fooled away his soul, and sinned away eternal life. And I am sure this is the next (most direct) way to do it; namely, to be slothful; slothful, I say, in the work of salvation ...
>
> If you would know a sluggard in the things of heaven, compare him with one that is slothful in the things of this world. As 1. He that is slothful is loth to set about the work he should follow: so is he that is slothful for heaven. 2. He that is slothful is one that is willing to make delays: so is he that is slothful for heaven. 3. He that is a sluggard, any small matter that cometh in between, he will make it a sufficient excuse to keep him off from plying his work: so it is also with him that is slothful for heaven. 4. He that is slothful doth his work by the halves; and so it is in him that is slothful for heaven ... 5. They that are slothful, do usually lose the season in which things are to be done: and thus it is also with them that are slothful for heaven, they miss the season of grace. And therefore, 6. They that are slothful have seldom or never good fruit; so also it will be with the soul-sluggard. 7. They that are slothful they are chid (rebuked) for the same: so also will Christ deal with those that are not active for him ...
>
> Arise man, be slothful no longer; set foot, and heart, and all into the way of God, and run, the crown is at the end of the race; there also standeth the loving forerunner, even Jesus, who hath prepared heavenly provision to make thy soul welcome, and he will give it thee with a more willing heart than ever thou canst desire it of him ...
>
> I wish our souls may meet with comfort at the journey's end.

This is the true, heartsearching, heartwarming John Bunyan, on full throttle, as indeed he is throughout this book. Let me not keep you from him, or him from you, any longer. As he says, heaven beckons: may we ever be found running for it.

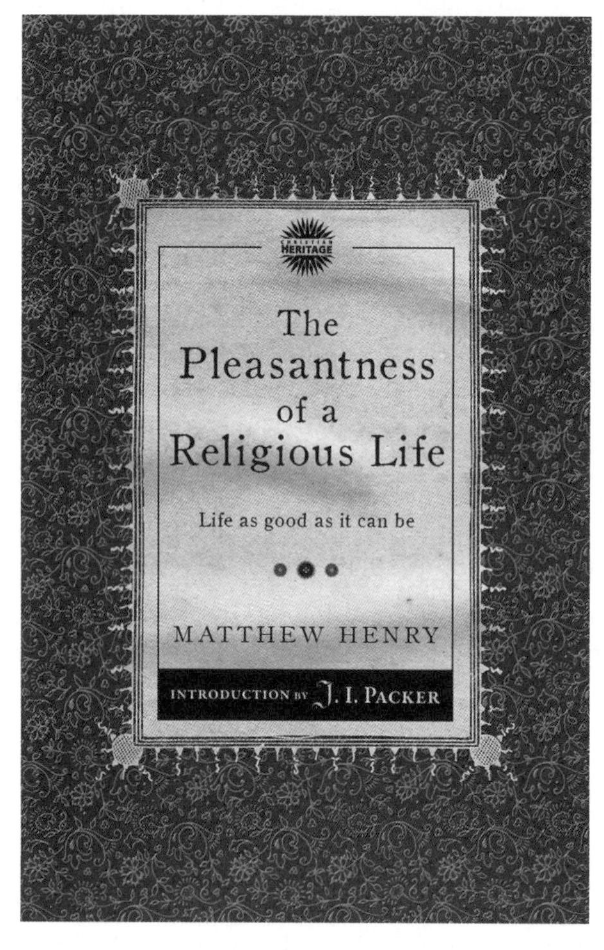

ISBN 978-1-84550-651-3

4

Matthew Henry

The Pleasantness of a Religious Life

I

This write-up of a set of six sermons was Matthew Henry's final literary labour. It was in the press when he died, aged 52, in 1714, and came out shortly after as *The Pleasantness of a Religious Life opened, and proved, and recommended to the consideration of all, particularly of Young People*. J.B. Williams, Henry's biographer, called this an 'attractive title', but I doubt whether many today will find it attractive.

That however is not Henry's fault. The reason this title strikes us as leaden-footed is that during the almost three centuries separating him from us 'pleasantness' has become a weak word, stating only that something is not too bad; 'religious' has become a vague word, covering all faiths and attitudes that involve 'God' or 'gods' (or, nowadays, 'goddesses') at some point; 'consideration' has become a cool word, suggesting thought that is consciously detached rather than committed; and 'young people' has become a patronizing phrase that creates expectations of being talked down to and so turns real young people off. If, however, the latter-day associations of Henry's title discourage us from digging into his book, it will be a pity; for what he is actually writing about, in his smooth, fulsome, and turn-of-the-seventeenth-century style is, the joy of Christian life, and as I usher his book back from obscurity into a world that has welcomed volumes on the joy of cooking and of sex and such like, I cannot help wishing that he had given it that kind of title.

Henry is quite up-front about what he is doing. Working from Proverbs 3:17, which the NIV renders '(wisdom's) ways are pleasant ways, and all her paths are peace,' he first observes that 'nothing draws more forcibly than pleasure', and then lays it down that 'true piety has true pleasure in it'. More fully:

> Pleasure is a tempting thing. What yields delight cannot but attract desire... religion has pleasure on its side... Here is a bait that has no hook under it... a pleasure which God himself invites you to, and which will make you happy, truly and eternally happy... it is certain that there is true pleasure in true religion (p. 49f.).

Henry's aim is to make us see that real Christianity is a journey into joy, always moving us on from one joy to another, and that this is one of many good and strong reasons for being excited and wholehearted in our discipleship. He makes his point well, and this is how:

First, he lists twelve pleasures that Christians as such enjoy: (1) knowing God and the Lord Jesus Christ; (2) resting in God; (3) being God's child; (4) tasting God's gracious goodness in all creature comforts; (5) relying on God's care; (6) delighting in God; (7) praising God; (8) escaping slavery to our appetites and (9) passions; (10) loving and doing good to others; (11) communing with God constantly; (12) looking forward to heaven's glory.

Then he reviews what God has done to bring sinners joy: made peace for them through the cross; promised them peace plus pleasure; and given them the Holy Spirit, the Scriptures, the ordinances of worship in prayer and song, and the gospel ministry, to bring home to them the blessings prepared for them. He lists those blessings as pardon, assurance, access to God, contentment, the calmness and confidence of a good conscience, and actual foretastes of glory.

Then he confirms what he has said so far by appealing to the facts of Christian experience, which fully verify his argument, and by picturing the Christian life as a journey made pleasant by its worth-whileness, by the gift of strength for travel, by the presence of the Holy Spirit to guard and guide, by good company, delightful terrain, good weather, and ample provisions en route, and by knowing that we shall experience journey's end as home.

Finally, having dismissed the scepticism of the irreligious and the misrepresentations of the morose regarding the delights of devotion, and having countered the idea that the pains of repenting, the demands of self-discipline and self-denial, and the constant experience of opposition, destroy the joy of discipleship, he urges his readers directly, starting from where they are, to enter into the fulness of the spiritual life that he has been describing.

Some things do not change. What Henry wrote nearly three centuries ago, wrapping it up in language that must strike us as old-fashioned, is as true and wise today as ever it was. We too get told, sometimes by our secular friends, sometimes by our own morbid thoughts, that being a Christian is a bleak and burdensome business, and not being a Christian would be more fun; we too, like Henry's first hearers and readers, need to be reminded that it is absolutely not so. Henry's reminder comes from his heart: 'herein, I confess,' he writes, 'I indulge an inclination of my own; for this doctrine of the pleasantness of religion is what I have long had a particular kindness for, and taken all occasions to mention' (p. 20). Christian life, though not a joy ride, is a joy road! As a connoisseur and veteran of spiritual pleasures, Henry will help us verify that today.

II

Who was Matthew Henry, who wrote this precious little book? He was a Silver Age Puritan. Let me explain.

In the world of literary study and history of ideas, a distinction is often drawn between the Golden and Silver Ages of creative movements. The Golden Age is the period in which the pioneers do the creative work, establishing themselves as the masters by the classical, landmark quality of their achievements. The Silver Age follows: it is a period in which those who lead seek first and foremost to follow in the footsteps of the forerunners, laying out, polishing up, and faithfully passing on the tradition of wisdom they have inherited. They dot its i's and cross its t's and develop its details as they go along, and, standing on their predecessors' shoulders, they sometimes top them in clarity and precision of statement; yet they remain conservers rather than creators, and settlers rather than explorers. Their goal is to maintain a heritage, and it is to this end that they dedicate their powers and devote their efforts.

In Christianity, the Golden-Silver distinction applies in different ways, according to one's angle of vision. Thus, from one standpoint you can label Luther's volcanically creative career as the Golden Age of the Reformation, and see the systematizing skill of Calvin and Melanchthon as its Silver counterpart. From another standpoint, the era of Luther, Calvin, Bucer, Martyr, Cranmer, Knox and their colleagues is the Golden Age of reformational theology, and the Puritan theological century from Perkins to Owen, with its continental counterpart from Beza to Turretin, is the Silver Age that succeeded it. From a third standpoint, master teachers of the Christian life like John Newton, Murray McCheyne, C.H. Spurgeon, J.C. Ryle, and Arthur Pink are the Silver Age in relation to the Golden Age of Puritan pioneers such as Perkins, Sibbes, Baxter, Bunyan, Owen, Gurnall, Thomas Goodwin and Thomas Hooker, for mapping the inner realities of the Christian life of faith, hope, and love. And from a fourth standpoint three men whose best work adorns the early eighteenth century should be seen as Silver Age figures in relation to the entire theological and practical output of the Puritan Golden Age that preceded them: namely, Cotton Mather, Isaac Watts, and Matthew Henry. All three are under-appreciated and need to be revalued, but here our focus is on Henry alone.

He was born in 1662, the year in which his godly Puritan father, Philip Henry, was one of two thousand ejected from pastoral ministry in the restored Church of England. His parents grounded him in Puritan beliefs and behaviour patterns (daily prayer, Bible reading, self-watch and self-examination; journal-keeping, and practice of the presence of God; scrupulous morality and generous philanthropy; thorough-going Sabbatarianism, and hard work for the other six days of the week). Precocious, bright, lively and Bible-loving, he never wanted to do anything else with his life other than serve his Lord in pastoral ministry; and in 1687, having passed through a nonconformist academy and read some law in Gray's Inn, he received Presbyterian ordination and began pastoring a congregation in Chester. It grew to over three hundred fifty during the twenty-five years he served it. In 1712, two years before his death, he relocated in Hackney, just outside London.

As a good preacher of the Puritan type, he was much in demand. As a matter of conscience he never refused an invitation to preach if he could possibly accept it, and throughout his ministry he was constantly in some pulpit or other, sometimes three times a day in different places.

Both Sunday services in his own church lasted up to three hours, since he not only preached for an hour from a text but also spent an hour expounding a chapter of the Bible. Out of this practice grew his famous Commentary, which he began to publish in 1704, and of which he completed five volumes, taking him to the end of Acts, before his death. (Friends later composed volume six on the basis of his surviving notes.)

Simple and practical in style while thoroughly scholarly and well-informed for substance, the Commentary remains an all-time classic, standing head and shoulders above any other popular exposition produced either before or since.

III

How should modern readers tune in to *The Pleasantness of a Religious Life*, in order to get the best out of it? This is a necessary question, for Henry assumes much that cannot be taken for granted today, and unless we adjust to this at the outset we may well be left feeling that his material is bland and facile, and does not really speak to our condition – or, putting it more bluntly, that you need to be a pretty old-fashioned person to appreciate such old-fashioned stuff! The following points are made in hope of pre-empting any such reaction.

First, we must get clear on the Puritan understanding of Christianity: which is a connected view of God, of the Bible, of the world, of ourselves, of salvation, of the church, of history and of the future. Few, it seems, even in Bible-believing churches, grasp this whole picture, and in liberal churches, where attention to scholars' fads and fancies replaces the teaching of the Bible, there is virtually no grasp of it at all. Once, churches taught it to all their children, using catechisms, but not any more. I state it here, therefore, in summary form.

God, who within the unity of His being is intrinsically a society, the Father, the Son, and the Holy Spirit together, and who is infinite, unchanging, and almighty in His wisdom, goodness, and justice, created the universe and ourselves within it, so that He might love and bless us, and we might love and praise Him. But things have gone wrong.

Original sin is the radical distortion of every human being's moral nature, making love and honour to God from our hearts impossible and self-centredness at deepest level inevitable. We sin because we are sinners, and human history, from one standpoint, is original sin writ large.

Jesus Christ the Saviour, the Jew who died, rose, reigns and will return for retribution to everyone, past, present and future, is God the Son incarnate, whose death atoned for our sins, whom we trust for forgiveness and acceptance and serve as our living Lord, and who unites us to Himself for the renewal of His image in us, dethroning original sin and giving us resources against its down-drag in the process. This is present salvation.

The Holy Spirit, the third divine person, acts for the Father and the Son by convincing us of our sin and need of Christ's reality as Saviour; by drawing us to Him in penitent faith through regeneration; by witnessing to our pardon, adoption and hope of glory; and by progressively working in us Christlikeness of character as we pursue what is in truth our journey home. This is the application of redemption.

The church is the supernatural society of all regenerate persons united by the Holy Spirit to Jesus Christ, called to worship, witness and work together for Christ's glory, and enriched with stated pastors, sacramental ordinances, and abundant serving abilities, for that purpose. Every Christian belongs to the church as God knows it, needs it as his supportive family, and should fellowship within it committedly in one of its particular local expressions. Christian life is corporate life.

The Bible, the written Word of God, is the divine source of knowledge of these things.

Such, in a nutshell, is the Puritan understanding of Christianity, which Henry assumes in his readers.

Second, we must get clear on the antithesis between Puritan Christianity and Western secularism, in both its modernist and post-modernist forms. Where Puritanism looks to the Word of God for self-knowledge and life-guidance, modernity looks with optimism to human reason as expressed in the sciences and philosophies, while post-modernism, of which today's universities are full, tells the modernists with pessimism that their enterprise is hopeless, since what philosophers and scientists, like Christians before them, offer as universal truth is really only an improper venture in mind-control.

Whatever be thought of this claim (does it, for instance, apply to post-modernism itself?), it is clearly as much an expression of secularism as is the modernity it seeks to undermine, and from the battlefield where modernists and post-modernists slug it out, the fumes of relativism, scepticism, and despair drift everywhere, producing a mind-set in which nothing seems certain, nothing feels quite worthwhile, and grabbing such pleasures as each moment offers seems the only thing to do. So human nature is devalued, human life is cheapened, human thought is blocked, and we live aimlessly, prompted only by instinct, appetite and various forms of greed in the manner of what we used to call the lower animals. Our idea of life is of drifting along, and our idea of pleasure stops short at the momentary satisfying of instinctual, sensual, body-based, self-absorbed cravings, urges and itches. (I grade these according to their strength: an urge is a strong itch, and a craving is a strong urge). This is where our secularism has brought us, and it is a sad story.

In direct antithesis to all aspects of this secular trend stands Henry's forceful recall to the eternal truth – 'true truth', as Francis Schaeffer would have said – about human nature.

> The soul is the man.... ['soul' here means personal, conscious, thinking, continuing self]. I hope it will be readily granted me, that man is principally to be considered as an intellectual, immortal being, endued with spiritual powers and capacities, allied to the world of spirits; that there is a spirit in man, which has sensations and dispositions of its own, active and receptive faculties, distinct from those of the body: and that this is the part of us, which we are, and ought to be most concerned about; because it is really well or ill with us, according as it is well or ill with our souls. Believe, that in our present state, the soul and the body have separate and contesting interests; the body thinks it is in its interest to have its appetites gratified, and to be indulged in its pleasures; while the soul knows it is in its interest to have the appetites of the body subdued and mortified, that spiritual pleasures may be the better relished.... Be wise, therefore; be resolute, and shew yourselves men who

> are actuated and governed by reason, and are affected by things as reason represents them to you: not reason as it is in the mere natural man, clouded and plunged and lost in sense; but reason elevated and guided by divine revelation to us and divine grace in us. Walk by faith, and not by sense (p. 50f.).

Only as we grasp the antithesis between the historic Christian and modern secular approaches to the business of living, and programme ourselves to shake off cultural prejudice and take the Christian, biblical, Puritan view of human nature and human welfare seriously, shall we be able to profit from the flood of wisdom that Henry here pours out as he gets into his stride.

The popular idea of a Puritan has always been of a pharisaical sourpuss who spreads gloom wherever he goes. In fact, however, as the real-life Puritan practised the disciplines of serious Christianity, praying, fasting, keeping his heart, warring against the world, the flesh and the devil, maintaining an ordered life and doing all the good he could, he found mental pleasure and joy at every turn of the road – in quiet, in tumult, in peace and prosperity, in sorrow and strain – and this is the experience that Henry wants to share and deepen. Thought-control, in realising the reality of God present each moment to bless, is the secret, and Henry's discourse, read and re-read, can lead us directly into it. I hope that very many will prove this to be so.

ISBN 978-1-84550-977-4

5

John Owen

The Mortification of Sin

I owe more, I think, to John Owen than to any other theologian, ancient or modern, and I am sure I owe more to his little book on mortification than to anything else he wrote. Let me explain.

I was converted – that is, I came to the Lord Jesus Christ in a decisive commitment, needing and seeking God's pardon and acceptance, conscious of Christ's redeeming love for me and his personal call to me – in my first university term, a little more than half a century ago. The group nurturing me was heavily pietistic in style, and left me in no doubt that the most important thing for me as a Christian was the quality of my walk with God: in which, of course, they were entirely right. They were also, however, somewhat elitist in spirit, holding that only Bible-believing evangelicals could say anything worth hearing about the Christian life, and the leaders encouraged the rest of us to assume that anyone thought sound enough to address the group on this theme was sure to be good. I listened with great expectation and excitement to the preachers and teachers whom the group brought in week by week, not doubting that they were the top devotional instructors in Britain, perhaps in the world. And I came a cropper.

Whether what I thought I heard was what was really being said may be left an open question, but it seemed to me that what I was being told was this. There are two sorts of Christians, first-class and second-class, 'spiritual' and 'carnal' (a distinction drawn from the King James rendering of 1 Cor. 3:1-3). The former know sustained peace and joy, constant inner confidence, and regular victory over temptation and sin, in a way that the latter do not. Those who hope to be of use to God must become 'spiritual' in the stated sense. As a lonely, nervy, adolescent introvert whose new-found assurance had not changed his temperament overnight, I had to conclude that I was not 'spiritual' yet. But I wanted to be useful to God. So what was I to do?

'Let go, and let God'

There is a secret, I was told, of rising from carnality to spirituality, a secret mirrored in the maxim: Let go, and let God. I vividly recall a radiant clergyman in an Oxford pulpit enforcing this. The secret had to do with being Spirit-filled. The Spirit-filled person, it was said, is taken out of the second half of Romans 7, understood (misunderstood, I would now maintain) as an analysis of constant moral defeat through self-reliance, into Romans 8, where he walks confidently in the Spirit and is not so defeated. The way to be Spirit-filled, so I gathered, was as follows.

First, one must *deny self.* Did not Jesus require self-denial from His disciples (Luke 9:23)? Yes, but clearly what He meant was the negating of carnal self – that is to say self-will, self-assertion, self-centredness and self-worship, the Adamic syndrome in human nature, the egocentric behaviour pattern, rooted in anti-God aspirations and attitudes, for which the common name is original sin. What I seemed to be hearing, however, was a call to deny *personal* self, so that I could be taken over by Jesus Christ in such a way that my present experience of thinking and willing would become something different, an experience of Christ Himself living in me, animating me and doing the thinking and willing for me. Put like that, it sounds more like the formula of demon-possession than the ministry of the indwelling Christ according to the New Testament. But in those days I knew nothing about demon-possession, and what I have just put into words seemed to be the plain meaning of 'I live; yet not I, but Christ liveth in me' (Gal. 2:20, KJV) as expounded by the approved speakers. We used to sing this chorus:

O to be saved from myself, dear Lord,
O to be lost in thee;
O that it may be no more I
But Christ who lives in me!

Whatever its author may have meant, I sang it whole-heartedly in the sense spelled out above.

The rest of the secret was bound up in the double-barrelled phrase *consecration and faith.* Consecration meant total self-surrender, laying one's all on the altar, handing over every part of one's life to the lordship of Jesus. Through consecration one would be emptied of self, and the empty vessel would then automatically be filled with the Spirit so that Christ's power within one would be ready for use. With consecration was to go faith, which was explained as looking to the indwelling Christ moment by moment, not only to do one's thinking and choosing in and for one, but also to do one's fighting and resisting of temptation. Rather than meet temptation directly (which would be fighting in one's own strength), one should hand it over to Christ to deal with, and look to Him to banish it. Such was the consecration-and-faith technique as I understood it – heap powerful magic, as I took it to be, the precious secret of what was called victorious living.

But what happened? I scraped my inside, figuratively speaking, to ensure that my consecration was complete, and laboured to 'let go and let God' when temptation made its presence felt. At that time I did not know that Harry Ironside, sometime pastor of Moody Memorial Church, Chicago, once drove himself into a full-scale mental breakdown through trying to get into the higher life as I was trying to get into it; and I would not have dared to conclude, as I have concluded since, that this higher life as described is a will-o'-the-wisp, an unreality that no one has ever laid hold of at all, and that those who testify to their experience in these terms really, if unwittingly, distort what has happened to them. All I knew was that the expected experience was not coming. The technique was not working. Why not? Well, since the teaching declared that everything depends on consecration being total, the fault had to lie in me. So I must scrape my inside again to find whatever maggots of unconsecrated selfhood still lurked there. I became fairly frantic.

And then (thank God) the group was given an old clergyman's library, and in it was an uncut set of Owen, and I cut the pages of volume VI more or less at random, and read Owen on mortification – and God used what the old Puritan had written three centuries before to sort me out. Here was God's chemo for my cancered soul.

Reaching across those three centuries, Owen showed me my inside – my heart – as no one had ever done before. Sin, he told me, is a blind, anti-God, egocentric energy in the fallen human spiritual system, ever fomenting self-centred and self-deceiving desires, ambitions, purposes, plans, attitudes, and behaviours. Now that I was a regenerate believer, born again, a new creation in Christ, sin that formerly dominated me had been de-throned but was not yet destroyed. It was marauding within me all the time, bringing back sinful desires that I hoped I had seen the last of, and twisting my new desires for God and godliness out of shape so that they became pride-perverted too. Lifelong conflict with the besetting sins that besetting sin generates was what I must expect.

What to do? Here was Owen's answer, in essence: Have the holiness of God clear in your mind. Remember that sin desensitises you to itself. Watch – that is, prepare to recognise it, and search it out within you by disciplined, Bible-based, Spirit-led self-examination. Focus on the living Christ and His love for you on the cross. Pray, asking for strength to say 'no' to sin's suggestions and to fortify yourself against bad habits by forming good ones contrary to them. And ask Christ to kill the sinful urge you are fighting, as the theophanic angel in C.S. Lewis's *The Great Divorce* tells the man with the lizard to do.

Does it work? Yes. Nearly seventy years on, I can testify to that.

Does Owen's book minster to others as it ministered to me? Yes. From prison just recently came the following:

> I found this book ... near a toilet on the floor .... Immediately after I finished reading Owen's *Mortification of Sin* I got on my knees on the floor of my cell and begged for Jesus to come into my miserable life and redeem me ... and for the first time in my entire life I meant every single word that I professed .... Thank you, Jesus!

Owen is one of the dead who still speak.

A Puritan Giant

Owen was by common consent the weightiest Puritan theologian, and many would bracket him with John Calvin and Jonathan Edwards as one of the three greatest Reformed theologians of all time. Born in 1616, he entered Queen's College, Oxford, at the age of twelve and secured his M.A. in 1635, when he was nineteen. In his early twenties, conviction of sin threw him into such turmoil that for three months he could scarcely utter a coherent word on anything; but slowly he learned to trust Christ, and so found peace. In 1637 he became a pastor; in the 1640s he was chaplain to Oliver Cromwell, and in 1651 he was made Dean of Christ Church, Oxford's largest college. In 1652 he was given the additional post of

Vice-Chancellor of the University, which he then reorganised with conspicuous success. After 1660 he led the Independents through the bitter years of persecution till his death in 1683.

He was a conservative Reformed theologian of great learning and expository strength. His thoughts are like the pillars of a Norman cathedral; they leave an impression of massive grandeur precisely because of their solid simplicity. He wrote for readers who, once they take up a subject, cannot rest till they see to the bottom of it, and who find exhaustiveness of coverage and presentation of the same truths from many different angles not exhausting but refreshing. His books have been truly described as a series of theological systems, each organised round a different centre. The truth of the Trinity – the story of the triune Creator becoming the triune Redeemer – was always his final point of reference, and the living of the Christian life was his constant concern.

Owen embodied all that was noblest in Puritan devotion. 'Holiness gave a divine lustre to his other accomplishments,' said his former junior colleague, David Clarkson, preaching at Owen's funeral. As a preacher, Owen bowed before his own maxim, that 'a man preacheth that sermon only well unto others which preacheth itself in his own soul', and declared: 'I hold myself bound in conscience and in honour, not even to imagine that I have attained a proper knowledge of any one article of truth, much less to publish it, unless through the Holy Spirit I have had such a taste of it, in its spiritual sense, that I may be able, from the heart, to say with the psalmist, "I have believed, and therefore have I spoken".' This explains the authority and skill with which Owen probes the dark depths of the human heart. 'Whole passages flash upon the mind of the reader with an influence that makes him feel as if they had been written for himself alone' (Andrew Thomson). The treatise on mortification is a signal example of this.

Wisdom on Mortification

Owen's 'discourse', as he called it, is a written-up set of pastoral sermons on Romans 8:13, KJV, 'If ye through the Spirit do mortify the deeds of the body ye shall live.' The sermons were preached in Oxford and the work was published in 1656 (second enlarged edition, 1658). It has been said of Jane Austen's novels that they should be read first for the fourth time, meaning that only fourth time around will their special excellences of balanced structure, gentle satire and subtle humour come into focus in the reader's mind. The same could be said of these sermons, for only through repeated reading is their searching power and unction adequately felt. Their theme is the negative side of God's work of sanctification (that is, character renewal in Christ's image). Reformed teachers from Calvin on have regularly explained the Holy Spirit's sanctifying work in terms of the positive, vivification (developing virtues), and the negative, mortification (killing sins). As the Westminster Confession (13:1) puts it:

> They, who are once effectually called, and regenerated, having a new heart, and a new spirit created in them, are further sanctified, really and personally, through the virtue of Christ's death and resurrection, by his Word and Spirit dwelling in them: the dominion of the whole body of sin is destroyed, and the several lusts thereof are more and more weakened and mortified, and they more and more quickened and strengthened in all saving graces, to the practice of true holiness, without which no man shall see the Lord.

Mortification is Owen's subject, and he is resolved to explain from Scripture the theology of it – that is, God's will, wisdom, work and ways regarding it – as fully as he can. But to make his treatment as practical and useful as possible, he addresses within the frame of his text the following question:

> Suppose a man to be a true believer, and yet finds in himself a powerful indwelling sin, leading him captive to the law of

> it, consuming his heart with trouble, perplexing his thoughts, weakening his soul as to duties of communion with God, disquieting him as to peace, and perhaps defiling his conscience and exposing him to hardening through the deceitfulness of sin, – what shall he do? what course shall he take and insist on for the mortification of this sin, lust, distemper or corruption...?

He then arranges his material as a series of things to know, and things to do, which between them answer the question as posed.

I spoke earlier of how Owen saved my spiritual sanity. I do in fact think, after sixty-plus years, that Owen has contributed more than anyone else to make me as much of a moral, spiritual and theological realist as I have so far become. He searched me to the root of my being. He taught me the nature of sin, the need to fight it and the method of doing so. He made me see the importance of the thoughts of the heart in one's spiritual life. He made clear to me the real nature of the Holy Spirit's ministry in and to the believer, and of spiritual growth and progress and of faith's victory. He showed me how to understand myself as a Christian and live before God humbly and honestly, without pretending either to be what I am not or not to be what I am. And he made every point by direct biblical exegesis, bringing out the experimental implications of didactic and narrative texts with a precision and profundity that I had not met before, and have rarely seen equalled since. The decisive dawning of all the insight I have ever received from Owen came, however, when first I read him on mortification. This small work is a spiritual gold mine. I cannot commend it highly enough.

Tuning In

I realise, however, as I write this that some readers will find it hard to tune in, so to speak, on Owen's wavelength, not just because his stately Latinised English with its fulsome rhetoric and occasional odd word trips them up, but because they suffer from the shortcomings of much present-day Christian nurture. Four of these in particular call for mention here.

First, *the holiness of God* is insufficiently emphasised. In Scripture, and in Owen, the holiness of 'the holy one' is constantly underlined. Holiness, which has been called the attribute of all God's attributes, is the quality that sets the Creator apart from His creatures, making Him different from us in our weakness, awesome and adorable to us in His strength, and a visitant to our consciences whose presence exposes and condemns sin within us. Too often today, however, God's holiness is played down, with the result that His love and mercy are sentimentalised and we end up thinking of Him as we would think of a kindly uncle. One effect of this unrealism is to make it hard for us to believe that the holy God of the Bible writers – prophets, psalmists, historians, apostles and very clearly the Lord Jesus Christ Himself – is the real God with whom we really have to deal. But the Puritans believed this, and an adjustment here must be made in our minds if we are to appreciate Owen's theology.

Second, *the significance of motivating desire* is insufficiently emphasised. In Scripture, and in Owen, desire is the index of one's heart, and the motivation is the decisive test of whether actions are good or bad. If the heart is wrong, lacking reverence, or love, or purity, or humility, or a forgiving spirit, but instead festering with pride, self-seeking ambition, envy, greed, hatred, sexual lust or the like, nothing that one does can be right in God's sight, as Jesus told the Pharisees time and time again. Too often today, however, as among the Pharisees, the moral life is reduced to role-play, in which prescribed and expected performance is everything and no attention is paid to the cravings, ragings and hostilities of the heart so long as people do what it is thought they should. This externalism, however, by which we assess ourselves, is not God's way of assessing us, and when Scripture tells Christians to mortify sin, the meaning is not just that bad habits must be broken, but that sinful desires and urgings must have the life drained out of them – which is what Owen is concerned to help us with throughout his book. An adjustment of outlook must be made here too if we are to appreciate Owen's thrust.

Third, *the need for self-scrutiny* is insufficiently emphasised. In Scripture, and in Owen, much stress is laid on the deceitfulness of the fallen human heart, and the danger of self-ignorance, with the result that one thinks well of one's heart and life when God, the searcher of hearts, is displeased with both. It is supremely ironical that in an era in which professional mind-doctors make so much of hidden and unrealised motivations, Christians should so regularly and resolutely decline to suspect themselves or each other of any form of self-deception in their ideas about themselves. Owen, a Puritan realist, knows that we are constantly fooling ourselves, or being fooled, with regard to our real attitudes and purposes, and hence insists that we must watch and examine ourselves by Scripture in order even to know what habits of our hearts need to be mortified. An adjustment in our mind-set has to be made here also if we are to appreciate Owen's probings.

Fourth, *the life-changing power of God* is insufficiently emphasised. In Scripture, and in Owen, subjective salvation means in the most literal sense a change of heart: a moral change that is rooted in a sustained exercise of faith, hope and love, whereby the power of Christ's death to deliver from domination by sinful desire, and the power of the Holy Spirit to induce Christlike attitudes and actions are constantly being proved. Mistaken as was the formula for supernatural living from which Owen delivered me, the expectation that Christians through prayer to Jesus would know deliverances from sinful passions in the heart was wholly right, and it is sad – indeed, scandalous – that today so little is heard about this, when so much is said about the power of Christ and His Spirit in various forms of ministry. But real deliverance from sinful passions is the blessing into which Owen would lead us, and he does not doubt that it is there to be had. 'Set faith at work on Christ for the *killing* of thy sin,' he writes. 'His blood is the great sovereign remedy for sin-sick souls. Live in this, and thou wilt die a conqueror; yea, thou wilt, through the good providence of God, live to see thy lust dead at thy feet.' Here, once more, an adjustment of our interest and expectancy must be made if we are to benefit from Owen's guidance.

Read on, then, with readiness to learn of the power of your Saviour and His Holy Spirit to set you free from your particular bondages to inordinate desire. God give us all hearts to understand and apply the truths that Owen sets forth here.

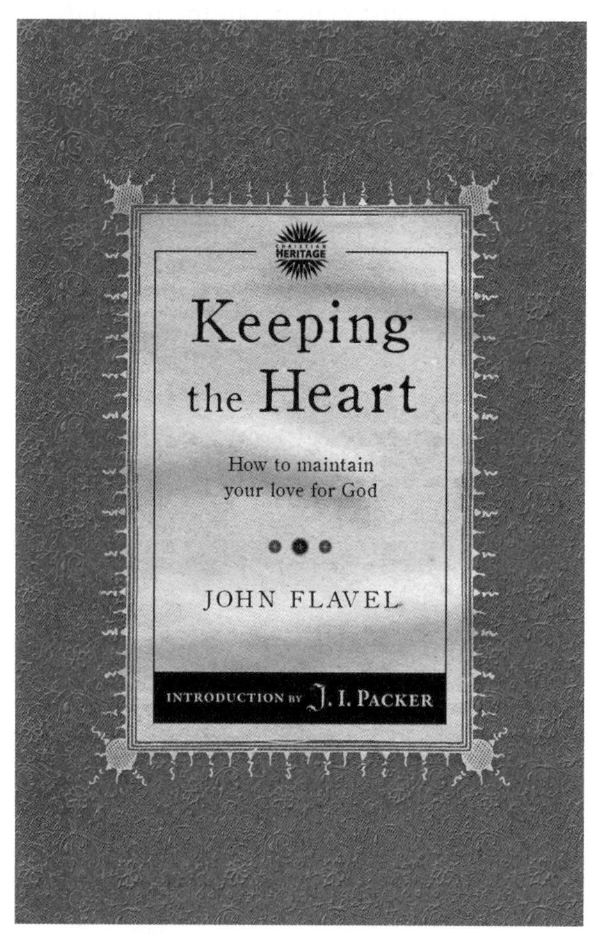

ISBN 978-1-84550-648-3

6

John Flavel

Keeping the Heart

I

'Heart-work and heaven-work' was Richard Baxter's crisp characterisation of real Christianity. John Flavel, with just about every other Puritan teacher, would be in total agreement. Real Christianity has in the past been conceived in terms of orthodoxy, orthopraxy, churchmanship, sacramentalism, syncretism, and various other things, but the Puritans as a body defined it precisely in terms of communion with God – more precisely still, communion with the triune Lord through Jesus Christ the Mediator. That is what the two phrases in Baxter's definition are pointing to. 'Heaven-work' signified a discipline of which Baxter himself was the supreme promoter, namely the practice of daily motivational meditation on the prospect of finally being with Christ in heaven. The purpose of this discipline was to keep the energy level of one's discipleship as high as possible, as one continued living the forward-tilted life (so we may fairly describe it) with the eyes of one's heart fixed on the ultimate destination. 'Heart-work' was a tag term for the admonitory thought and repeated self-search that were constantly needed to sustain the most ardent love and devotion to

Christ, and the firmest resistance to the many kinds of hostility and discouragement that in God's providence the Puritans had to face. John Flavel's *Keeping the Heart* (first published as *A Saint Indeed*) displays this finely, as we shall soon see.

What is the heart that Flavel, like Baxter, is talking about? The Puritan understanding of the heart is rooted, not in medical physiology, which knows the heart as a pump sending blood round the body, but in biblical theology and anthropology, which sees the heart as the central, dynamic core of personal life. The Bible uses the word in this way about a thousand times, and thereby highlights, illustrates and enforces the following truths:

(1) The human heart is the controlling source of all that we do in expression of what we are: all our thoughts, desires, discernments and decisions, our plans and purposes, our affections, attitudes and ambitions, all the wisdom and all the folly that mark our lives, come out of, and are fuelled, serviced and driven by, our hearts, for better or for worse. Our Lord Jesus showed Himself vividly aware of this. 'How can you speak good, when you are evil? For out of the abundance of the heart the mouth speaks' (Matt. 12:34). 'From within, out of the heart of man, come evil thoughts, sexual immorality, theft, murder, adultery, coveting, wickedness, deceit, sensuality, envy, slander, pride, foolishness. All these evil things come from within, and they defile a person' (Mark 7:21-23).

(2) The salvation that God gives us in Christ is rooted in a created and creative change of heart, as described by Ezekiel in an oracle about the restoring of Israel following the captivity: 'I will give you a new heart, and a new spirit I will put within you. And I will remove the heart of stone from your flesh and give you a heart of flesh. And I will put my Spirit within you, and cause you to walk in my statutes and be careful to obey my rules' (Ezek. 36:26-27). The new, renewed heart becomes, on the one hand, the source of faith in Christ and in the gospel promises, whereby we enter a new relationship of acceptance with God; and, on the other hand, the source of love to God and man – the grateful, responsive, resolute purpose of honouring and pleasing God in all things, and seeking the best for our nearest and dearest and whoever else may cross our path. The new heart, acting in

these ways, is in fact the sign of our salvation, and the inward discipline of sustaining such action is the reality of 'heart-work:' which, be it soberly said, is work indeed.

Saying this brings us to John Flavel and the book I am introducing. But before we look at the book, something should be said about the man himself.

II

A native of Bromsgrove in Worcestershire, Flavel was a preacher's son, and it does not appear that he ever wanted to be anything but a pastoral preacher himself. Born in 1628, he graduated from Oxford and became a pastor in 1650. The ministry for which he is remembered was located in Dartmouth, Devon, the port town to which he moved in 1656. He gained distinction as a preacher of the classic Puritan type, expository, analytical, didactic, applicatory, searching, converting and edifying, with divine unction regularly empowering his pulpit work. His writings reveal him as clear-headed and eloquent in the plain Puritan style, orthodox, Christ-focused and life-centred in his subject-matter, with his mind always set on advancing true godliness, with peace and joy in the Lord. It is recorded of him that he spent much time in meditation, self-examination and prayer, and on one occasion at least he had an extraordinary experience of God. Meditating on horseback, 'his thoughts began to swell and rise higher and higher like the waters in Ezekiel's vision till at last they became an overflowing flood. Such was the intention of his mind, such the ravishing tastes of heavenly joys, and such the full assurance of his interest therein, that he utterly lost a sight and sense of this world and all the concerns thereof, and for some hours he knew no more where he was than if he had been in a deep sleep upon his bed.' Stopping, exhausted, at a wayside pool, 'he sat down and washed, earnestly desiring, if it were God's pleasure, that it might be his parting place from this world. Death had the most amiable face in his eye that ever he beheld, except the face of Jesus Christ which made it so, and he could not remember, though he believed himself dying, that he had one thought of his dear wife and children or any other earthly concernment.' When he finally reached the inn to which he was heading, the innkeeper said to him, 'Sir, what is the matter with you? You look like a dead man' – to which Flavel replied, 'I was never better in my life.' At the inn, 'the influence still continued, banishing sleep. Still, still the joy of the Lord overflowed him, and he seemed to be an inhabitant of the other world. He many years after called that day one of the days of heaven.' One thinks of Paul, caught up to what he called the third heaven, and of Jonathan Edwards weeping as he walked through the woods by reason of the vividness with which he perceived the glory and beauty of God. Well may we pause in awe for a moment before moving on.

Flavel was ejected from his pulpit in 1662 as a nonconformist, following the re-establishment of the Church of England by the Act of Uniformity which itself followed the restoration of the monarchy in 1660. His people pressed him to continue his (now illegal) ministry to them, and this for two decades he did, preaching in private houses, in woodlands, on a rocky island in the Salcombe River estuary that was submerged at high tide, and in other places where the long arm of the law could be evaded. Then from 1682 to 1685 he joined with a Congregational church in London, assisting his friend William Jenkyn, commentator on Jude, who was its minister. Here, too, dodging arrest by the authorities (posses of soldiers sent out by the magistrates) was part of his way of life. When in 1687 James II lifted restrictions on nonconformist ministry, Flavel was already back in Dartmouth, and his still-loyal congregation at once erected a large church building in which his ministry could continue. He died in 1691, leaving a written legacy of biblical and devotional exposition that was first published as two large folios and that became 3,600 pages in six volumes in its 1968 reprint.

III

In *Keeping the Heart*, Flavel leads us into what, for him, is the most basic of all the disciplines of the Christian's inner life – basic to worship and prayer; basic to faith, hope and love; basic to humility, peace and joy; basic to pure-heartedness and steady obedience.

What discipline is this? It is the discipline that we may call *admonitory meditation*, that is, the deployment within one's own mind of key lines of thought that will confirm and reinforce the various aspects of faithful communion with God, and recall us to Him in renewed loyalty when we have slipped away, or been drawn away, from the path of faithfulness. Such slippages begin in the mind, and begin with the contemplation of actual or potential disorder, moral or circumstantial, without relating the matter to God, and the practice of *admonitory meditation* is, in effect, talking to oneself before the Lord, reminding oneself of truths about the ways of God and the grace of Christ that will energise and stabilise one for a return to, and continuance on, the path of faithfulness, no matter what. These truths, re-anchored in the heart by applicatory meditation, will stir believers to renew their prayers for strength to carry on through thick and thin. Flavel is vividly aware that sin and Satan are constantly alluring us to follow the gleam of unthinking blind desire, and he knows how vitally important it is to counter the away-from-God thoughts and moods that lay hold of us in a way that if not checked will ruin us. Most of *Keeping the Heart* is taken up with setting out the best lines of thought with which to sustain ourselves when thus tempted in life's various ups and downs.

Would I be wrong, I wonder, to guess that most of us nowadays do very little of this thoughtful inward arguing with ourselves in times of testing? We expect that when inward or outward circumstances expose us to temptation we shall recognise it straight away and be able to banish it with a simple 'no'. But in fact keeping the heart steady, zealous for God's glory and consciously close to Christ is not always so easily done, while our expectation that we shall be able to say 'no' when necessary without inward effort and struggle only shows how unrealistic we are, and how easily we are betrayed into doing wrong and foolish things believing them to be wise and right; how easily, too, we lapse into what T.S. Eliot called 'the ultimate treason: to do the right thing for the wrong reason'. Flavel makes it evident that for him there are no shortcuts here, and that blithe self-reliance in times of testing is the high road to spiritual suicide. May we absorb His wisdom as we sit at His feet.

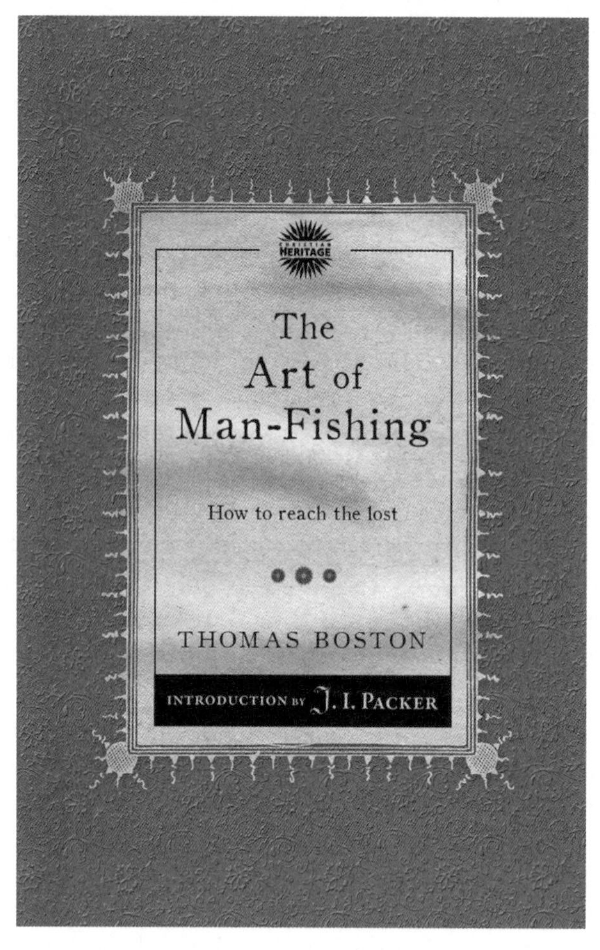

ISBN 978-1-78191-108-2

7a

Thomas Boston

The Art of Man-Fishing

I

In January, 1699, twenty-two-year old Thomas Boston, already a licenced preacher in the Church of Scotland though not yet a parish pastor, 'wrote a soliloquy on the art of man-fishing'. The soliloquy has the form of a sermonic meditation addressed to himself on Christ as his model for his ministry of the Word. In the memoirs which Boston edited for his children in 1730, as his life neared its end, he recalled how it happened.

> 6th January 1699, reading in secret, my heart was touched with Matt. iv. 19, 'Follow me, and I will make you fishers of men.' My soul cried out for accomplishing of that to me, and I was very desirous to know how I might follow Christ, so as to become a fisher of men; and for my own instruction in that point, I addressed myself to the consideration of it in that manner.... That scribble gives an idea of the then temper of my spirit...[1]

The 'scribble', so Boston tells us, was never finished (not that it leaves any sense of incompleteness when read today), and no one outside the family saw it till it was published in 1773. Since

1 *Memoirs of Thomas Boston* (Banner of Truth, 1988), p. 48.

then, however, it has been constantly hailed by evangelicals as a masterpiece on ministry, worthy to stand on the same shelf as Baxter's *Reformed Pastor*, and it is in those terms that I commend it now.

The idea of a beginner preacher of twenty-two producing a spiritual masterpiece is startling, no doubt. But Boston was an unusual man. He had been brought up by godly, conscientious Presbyterian parents (as a child he had on one occasion accompanied his father to jail for the latter's nonconformity). He had been soundly converted at age eleven, through the ministry of Henry Erskine, a veteran saint in his sixties who had been one of the two thousand Puritan clergy ejected in 1662 and who during the winter of 1687 was minister of a church four miles from Boston's home. His father took him to hear Erskine, a spiritual impact was made immediately, and then 'in the winter, sometimes it was my lot to go alone, without so much as the benefit of a horse to carry me through Blackadder water, the wading whereof in sharp frosty weather I very well remember. But such things were then easy, for the benefit of the word, which came with power.'[2] 'Sure I am, I was in good earnest concerned for a saving interest in Jesus Christ; my soul went out after him, and the place of his feet was glorious in my eyes.'[3] He and two other Christian boys from his school 'met frequently in a chamber in my father's house, for prayer, reading the Scriptures, and spiritual conference; whereby we had some advantage, both in point of knowledge and tenderness.'[4] Boston's lifelong habits of self-scrutiny, prayer, and Bible reading with systematic meditation, were formed at that time.

There is more to be said. As Boston had a sensitive spirit, so he had a first-class mind, a retentive memory, and a way with words. He was always a man who thought best with a pen in

---

2 p. 10.

3 *Ibid.*

4 p. 11.

his hands, writing out ideas and arguments as they came to him. He had matured early; his theological convictions were clear, his sense of call to a preaching and shepherding ministry was strong, and his insight into the vistas opened by biblical texts was already deep. The qualities that were later to lead Jonathan Edwards to describe him as 'a truly great divine' were already in evidence, and the power to speak to the heart that is sustained throughout his later and greater treatise, *The Fourfold State* (1720), was there too.

Put all of this together, and the star quality of *The Art of Man-Fishing*, while still breath-taking, becomes at least intelligible.

II

Boston was a mainstream Scottish Puritan (to use the word that fits; 'Puritan' was not used in Scotland as a label in the way it was in England). The Puritan type of faith and piety received its classic formulation in the Westminster Confession and Catechisms, which were the authorised standards of the Church of Scotland in Boston's day. It will help us to appreciate the pastoral theology of the *Art* if we remind ourselves of the main features of the Puritan outlook, as the Westminster documents display them.

The Westminster standards were drawn up by the veritable cream of English and Scottish clergy. Working in the middle years of the 1640s, they had behind them as resources and models, establishing perimeters, parameters, and trajectories for their thought, the sixteenth century Reformed confessions, including the Anglican 39 Articles which they were charged to supersede; the legacy of theological exposition that began with Calvin and Knox; more than a century of intense international debate, carried on in print, regarding Roman Catholic, Lutheran and Arminian deviations from Reformed views; dozens of catechisms produced by Puritan pastors and a great deal of catechising experience; much published exegetical and expository work on the biblical text, from both Catholic and Protestant scholars; and, last but not least, a mass of 'practical affectionate' English Puritan treatises on conversion and the inner devotional realities of the Christian life. Basic to Westminster's theological method was belief in the divinely inspired truth and coherence of the Bible, and a resolve to affirm only that which could be verified and vindicated from Scripture itself, as a faithful echo of God's own teaching. Drawing on the resources listed above, and hewing conscientiously at every point to the line of Scripture, Westminster theology was masterful in style as well as masterly in substance, and it is no wonder that it shaped Presbyterian and Reformed theology both sides of the Atlantic so decisively.

Westminster theology is trinitarian, and centres on the way in which mankind's Creator and Judge became mankind's Redeemer and Saviour through the outworking of a plan that casts Jesus Christ, the God-man, in the role of Mediator and the Holy Spirit, the Paraclete, in the role of the Life-giver. The plan is like an ellipse with two foci: focus one is the covenant of grace whereby, on the basis of Christ's righteousness and blood-shedding, relations between the Creator and His human creatures are restored; focus two is union with Christ by the Spirit in regeneration whereby fallen human nature is remade. In all of this the Lord Jesus Christ Himself, God incarnate who redeemed, rose, reigns, and will one day return to judgment, becomes the direct object of faith, hope, love and joy. The world-wide church, of which all Christian congregations are members, is the sphere of salvation as it maintains the ministry of the Word and sacraments and worships God according to His command. Christ is the Head of the church and through the Spirit the source of all its spiritual life, and the church must be the Christian's home as long as he is in this world. Such in a nutshell is the theology of Westminster.

Implicit, and sometimes explicit, in the Confession and Catechisms is the Puritan concept of conversion as a process that begins with awakening from spiritual complacency to spiritual unease as one faces the reality of one's sin, and leads on through questings for faith, repentance, and a new life with God, to a God-given confidence that one has been divinely enabled to turn from sin to a self-abandoning trust in Christ, the sin-bearer, as one's Lover, Lord, and Life, and that one's heart has been renewed in the process. Boston's idea of the minister as a 'fisher of men' is that through his public ministry in the pulpit and his private ministry of one-to-one admonition God will work in people's hearts to bring them to this place of settled commitment, where they can confirm their assurance of being alive to God by noting the ongoing change in their inner being.

Believing that the fallen human heart is desperately prone to optimistic self-deception, Westminster Puritans stressed the need for constant self-suspicion and self-examination. There was nothing of morbid introspection about this; on the contrary, it was experienced as a bracing and reassuring exercise, as the regenerate discerned within themselves the signs of life from the Holy Spirit. Boston, facing the fact that only those alive in Christ can follow Christ, himself takes time in the early pages of the *Art* to examine himself in this way.

> I think I have Spirit; that is, that I have life... from the following grounds... I have light that before I did not have.... This light lets me see my heart-sins... and is still discovering the baseness of my heart to me.... It makes me see Christ as precious... makes me trust in him... I lean on him for help in his own work... in temptations and trials, I endeavour to lift up my soul to him. I feel help... from the Spirit.... Many times I have gone to prayer very dead, and have come away with life... I find a threefold flame, though weak, in my heart. (a) A flame of love to Christ... I have a love to his truths... I love the promises... I love his threatenings as most just ... I love those in whom the image of God appears... I love his work... I love his ordinances... I love his glory, that he should be glorified, come of me what will. (b) I find in my heart a flame of desires toward the righteousness of Christ... My soul... acquiesces in justification by an imputed righteousness... Sometimes my soul longs... to be dissolved, and to be with Christ... (c) I find in my heart some heat of zeal for God... I move forward towards heaven... I am more acquainted with Christ and his ways than before... there is a growth of love in me... I can, I think, trust God more now than before...

> my soul is habitually more watchful than before. Nor do I dare give such liberty to my heart as sometimes I gave... I see growth of contempt of the world. And this, blessed be God, is on the increase in me (pp. 50ff.).

Evangelism was not a word that Boston knew, but evangelism, in the sense of awakening the unconverted to their need of Christ, leading them to faith and repentance, and establishing them in the new life to which his own self-analysis testifies, is what 'man-fishing' meant to him, and it was this skill that he sought to learn from the example of Jesus's own soul-winning service.

III

Puritan evangelism, as carried on by preaching and pastoral admonition, took time, and was expected to take time. Strong sudden impressions from God about particular spiritual issues would frequently occur as the Word of God was preached, but ministers in the Westminster tradition were realistic about the likelihood that the conversion process from start to finish would take months, just as the gestation and final birth of a human baby does. In this, men like Boston have an important lesson to teach us today. Since mass evangelism on neutral ground, led by a freelance who specialises in this particular activity, became a regular feature of the Christian scene, the concept of conversion as typically a short, sharp affair that can be precisely narrated and dated has become normative for evangelical minds. Clearly, its source is the evangelistic rally, where, after warming up and softening up preliminaries, the evangelist speaks of human sin and divine grace, appeals for commitment to Christ, and passes on those persuaded to counsellors, who help them to make their commitment firm. Our romantic imaginations are right to recognise receiving Jesus Christ as Saviour from the guilt and power of sin and Lord of one's life henceforth as the essence of conversion, but wrong to fancy that the whole process ordinarily starts and ends within an hour or two; just as we are wrong to imagine, as we sometimes do, that any happy results from the rally depend in a decisive way on the evangelist's special gifts and the quality of his performance.

Realism requires us to face the fact that though God may prompt special evangelistic ventures, and use them in a spectacular way to advance or complete the conversion process, that process usually has many other stages, in all of which the decisive factor is the sovereignty of God's grace. The main way in which God advances conversion, in our day as in Boston's, is through the sustained faithfulness of parents, friends, and church teachers witnessing, instructing, and encouraging informally, and of preachers expounding the gospel from Scripture in worship contexts. The first requirement, therefore, in the church's unending work of 'man-fishing' is that these activities go on incessantly, shaped by clear and serious purpose and backed by earnest importunity in prayer.

IV

Boston wrote the *Art* when he was a probationer preacher looking forward to a life of parochial ministry. Naturally, therefore, it was the demands, problems, and pitfalls of his present and future role that concerned him most, and the second half of the work is taken up with exploring what following Christ in faithful ministry involves. From this standpoint, the *Art* is a classic text which any minister of the word in any age might well use for an annual check-up. Certainly, we who preach will never get beyond its clear-sighted, challenging, searching wisdom, of which the following is a rough summary.

The call of God to shepherd His flock (says Boston) requires us to model ourselves on Jesus Christ, our Lord and Master, in at least the following particulars:

1. Faithfulness, even when it runs the risk of upsetting people and turning them against us. We must renounce the 'carnal policy' of trimmers and time-servers who tone

God's message down, and must present the realities of sin and grace forthrightly, rebuking where necessary, pulling no punches, and leaving the outcome to God.

2. Evangelistic purpose. 'Christ had the good of souls in his eye.... When you preach, let this be your design, to seek to recover lost sheep ... to get some converted, and brought in to your Master.'
3. Prayerfulness. Christ spent time and energy in prayer both before and after his preaching of the word, and we need to do the same.
4. Single-mindedness, free from any form of the personal profit motive.
5. Enterprise in usefulness. Jesus took every opportunity 'to instruct, rebuke, etc., from such things as offered,' both one to one and in larger companies. So must we: so 'learn the heavenly chemistry of extracting some spiritual things out of earthly things,' and 'do not refuse any occasion of preaching when God calls you to it.' 'If Christ should come and find you idle, when He is calling you to work, how will you be able to look him in the face? They are well that die at Christ's work.' These are the last words of the book.

A century and a half after Boston's time, another Scotsman, Horatius Bonar, wrote a powerful hortatory hymn on Christian ministry which, whether he realised it or not, capsules perfectly the admonitions of Boston's *Art*. My guess (which of course I cannot prove) is that he knew his Boston so well that he could not think of ministry save in Bostonian terms. His hymn is certainly another admirable text for the minister's periodic self-assessment, and the best way to end this introduction will be to quote it in full. This, then, is what Boston's message to us amounts to.

Go, labour on; spend and be spent;
Thy joy to do the Father's will;

It is the way the Master went:
Should not the servant tread it still?

Go, labour on while it is day;
The world's dark night is hastening on;
Speed, speed thy work; cast sloth away;
It is not thus that souls are won.

Toil on, faint not, keep watch, and pray;
Be wise the erring soul to win;
Go forth into the world's highway,
Compel the wanderer to come in.

Toil on, and in thy toil rejoice;
For toil comes rest, for exile home;
Soon shalt thou hear the Bridegroom's voice,
The midnight cry, 'Behold, I come!'

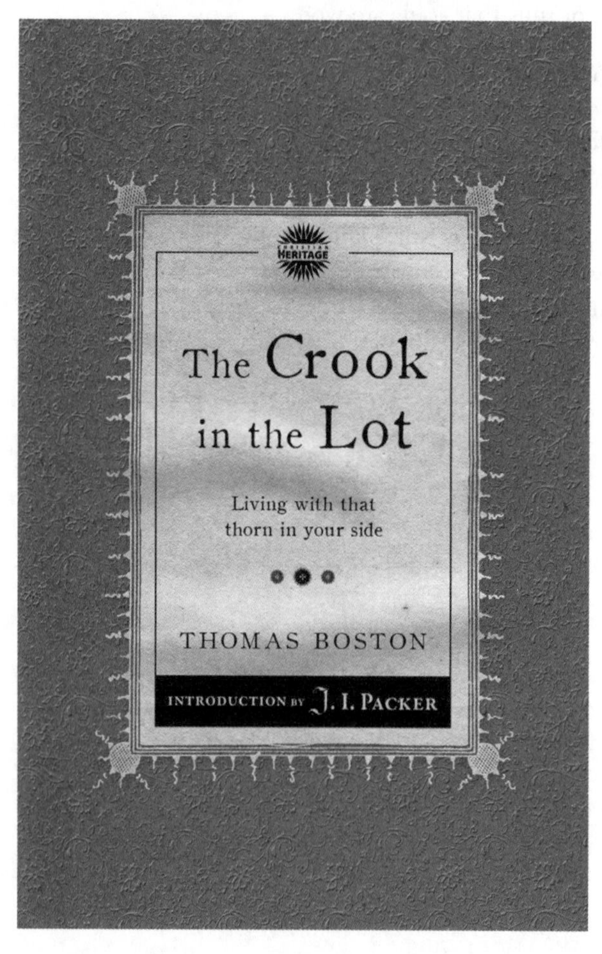

ISBN 978-1-84550-649-0

7 b

Thomas Boston

The Crook in the Lot

I

As an Englishman who has lived in North America for thirty-two years, during an era of rapid cultural change, I know more about how today's North Americans use words than I do about their British counterparts, so it may be that what I say in my next sentence would not apply so directly on the east side of the Atlantic. It is certain, however, that if a North American man in the street – say, the man on the Vancouver omnibus – heard a reference to the crook in the lot, he would think it must signify a criminal hiding out on a piece of probably undeveloped real estate (what Brits would call, property), and he would not be able to imagine what else it might mean. But in Thomas Boston's usage the *crook* is the crooked, that is the uncomfortable, discontenting aspects of a person's life, the things that the Puritans called losses and crosses, and that we speak of as the stones in our shoe, the thorns in our bed, the burrs under the saddle, and the complaints we have to live with; and the lot is the providentially appointed path that God sets each of His servants to travel. Boston, minister of Ettrick in south Scotland, who with Jonathan Edwards represents most brilliantly the prolonging into the eighteenth century of pure Puritanism, as a Bible-based, church-centred, faith-oriented, prayer-drenched movement of personal spiritual life, left at his death (he died in harness in 1732, aged fifty-six) a little treatise on this theme, which he had already begun to prepare for the press. His friends finished the job, and the work was published in 1737, under the title *The Crook in the Lot: The Sovereignty and Wisdom of God in the Afflictions of Men Displayed.* That is what is before you now.

The movie *Shadowlands* represented C. S. Lewis as an inexperienced theorist who pontificated in public regarding pain and grief without knowing anything about it until he lost his wife. This, no doubt, was good Hollywood, but the story of the real C. S. Lewis was very different, and so was the story of Thomas Boston. *The Crook in the Lot* emerged from what in his autobiography Boston called 'the groaning part of my life', the final eight years, during which, in addition to ongoing battles for the gospel against the non-evangelical leadership of the Church of Scotland and the continuance of his wife's paralyzing depression, he was a martyr to some form of the stone (gravel, he called it) and saw himself become a physical wreck. When he wrote and spoke of life's troubles he knew what he was talking about, and the sense that this was so comes through strongly, even though there is nothing directly autobiographical in the analysis that the treatise offers.

It began, as the reader can see, as seven sermons: three on Ecclesiastes 7:13, 'Consider the work of God; for who can make that straight which he hath made crooked?'; one on Proverbs 16:19, 'Better is it to be of an humble spirit with the lowly, than to divide the spoil with the proud'; and three on 1 Peter 5:6: 'Humble yourselves therefore under the mighty hand of God, that he may exalt you in due time'. Boston had an architectural mind (Jonathan Edwards hailed him as 'a truly great divine'), and he liked preaching series of sermons that illustrated key topics from a number of texts; he wrote out the sermons in his easy, flowing English as part of his preparation for preaching them; and here, as in his better-known *Fourfold*

State, the combination of perfect clarity with biblical light and weight searches the reader's heart and again and again makes us face ourselves on specific matters, impacting us with the sudden force of a depth-charge that explodes far below the surface level of our being. This is a way of saying that, as with Edwards and many of the Puritans of the previous century, divine unction rests on Boston's homiletical writing just as once it rested on his actual preaching; and that is a way of saying that the reality of the power of God in his own heart spilled over into his verbal communication. Be prepared, then, to find that God is preaching to you through Boston as you read *The Crook in the Lot*.

II

Two years before his death Boston wrote: 'I bless my God in Jesus Christ, that ever he made me a Christian, and took an early dealing with my soul [Boston came to faith at age eleven, under the preaching of Henry Erskine, a minister ejected from the Church of England in 1662], that ever he made me a minister of the gospel, and gave me true insight into the doctrine of his grace.' That 'true insight' which *The Crook in the Lot* presupposes, can be learned in detail from Boston's voluminous though very self-consistent output, studied as a whole; or from the Westminster Confession and Catechisms, where it is crystallised; but modern readers may not have time or inclination for this research, and their minds may already be possessed by different notions. So before going further I shall sketch out the frame of doctrine into which this little treatise fits. It is doctrine with a catechetical rather than an academic cast, in other words it is truth as one presents it to persons ignorant of Christianity in order to bring them to know, love, worship and serve God, and thus to make them true disciples of Jesus Christ.

1. The triune God, through whom we exist, in whose hands we always are, and who will in due course judge us and award us our final destiny, is totally sovereign over everything in His world, controlling even the free choices of human beings.

2. The human heart is naturally self-centred, self-deifying, self-serving, and unresponsive and hostile to God's claims, so that it leads everyone to live in a way which, if not changed, will bring final condemnation, rejection, retribution and separation from God's fellowship and love.

3. Jesus Christ, the incarnate Lord and Mediator, prophet, priest and king, crucified, risen and reigning, offers Himself to everyone in the gospel, inviting and commanding all who hear to receive and trust Him as the Saviour, Lord and Friend in and through whom they may be forgiven and restored and adopted into the Father's family for transformation into the image of the Son.

4. Through regeneration of heart by the Holy Spirit persons who seek Christ find Him, and by faith live new lives henceforth as His disciples, empowered by the Spirit who now indwells them.

5. In every disciple's life there are crooked things, unpleasant and unwelcome, which God uses to test us, strengthen us, humble us, correct us, teach us lessons, further our self-knowledge, repentance, and sanctity, shield us from greater evils, and thus bring us blessing, grievous as at first sight the crooked things seem to be.

6. The knowledge that in every case the crook in our lot belongs to this world only, and that again and again God delivers His people when they pray from particular afflictions that burden them here and now, should sustain believers as they undergo these divine chastenings, helping them to hold fast the certainty that 'all things work together for good for those who love God, who are called according to his purpose' (Rom. 8:28, NRSV).

These are the basic truths of which, at least in rough terms, Boston expects his readers to have some awareness. His treatise will remind us of many of them and amplify some of them in detail, but none is presented as a new idea, and evidently Boston sees his role as helping people to know better, and apply to themselves more thoroughly, things that in some sense they know already. Some of Boston's thoughts may be new to us, but that does not mean they were new to his own first hearers. It is clear that at catechetical level congregations were better taught in Boston's day than they are in ours – which, when you think of the way catechising has dropped out of church and family life, is hardly matter for surprise.

With these truths clear in our minds, however, we are equipped to tune in to *The Crook in the Lot* and, if I may put it this way, to suck sweetness out of it.

III

To this end I pose two questions.

First: what did Boston design the *Crook* to do, originally to his hearers at Ettrick and then to his readers, people such as ourselves? To what end did he select and arrange this material? What, pastorally, was his aim? Long ago I was taught that if you aim at nothing in particular you are sure to achieve it. What did Boston hope to achieve?

A partial answer would be: to teach people. It has been said that the three priorities in pastoral ministry are, first, to teach, second, to teach, and third, to teach, and Boston would have agreed with that. Preaching, as persons like himself in the Puritan tradition understood it, is teaching plus application, and the application is itself a didactic engagement of the mind before it is anything else. The rationale of this position is that all truth enters the heart via the understanding, and that authentic Christianity is essentially belief of and obedience to the revealed truth of God, and that the Bible itself is that truth, presented in a variety of forms – by narrative, by parable, by argumentation, by vision, and so on – but all, as Paul says, 'profitable for teaching, for reproof, for correction, for training in righteousness' (2 Tim. 3:16, NASB). Boston's teaching process enlarges biblical understanding in more than one way; the passages he gathers illuminate the truth they are cited to support, and that truth in turn illuminates the significance of these passages in their own context. The modern way to mark this fact is to applaud Boston for his skill in canonical interpretation, that is, his insight into the whole Bible, all sixty-six books of it in the two testamentary collections, as a theological unity setting forth in a wonderfully consistent and coherent manner the will, work and ways of God the Creator-become-Redeemer, plus the wisdom about God, the world, and life that the godly are called to learn. Like Calvin and the Puritans before him, Boston offers canonical interpretation of the Bible that in both spiritual and intellectual quality far outstrips most ventures in this field today. One supposes that depth of dependence on the Holy Spirit, who as inspirer of the Bible must ever be its ultimate interpreter, has something to do with this fact.

Boston's basic contention, which all his teaching here is concerned to make good, is that: 'A just view of afflicting incidents is altogether necessary to a Christian deportment under them; and that view is to be obtained only by faith, not by sense; for it is the ... Word alone that represents them justly, discovering in them the work of God, and consequently, designs becoming the divine perfections.' Assuming general knowledge of the plan of salvation as laid out above, he first shows us with piercing precision what constitutes a crook in one's lot (circumstances causing revulsion and complaint, and generating all the temptations of discontent), and he analyses for us what modes of crook there are (defects in our make up; dishonour, sometimes observed, sometimes not; lack of appropriate success in our endeavours; and bad relationships everywhere). Then he tells us how we should seek God's help to 'even' (straighten) the crooks, while humbling ourselves under them and acknowledging that some of them are here to stay while this life lasts. And finally he explains how we should focus our hope on the promised 'lifting up' that, here or hereafter, will be our experience. Points recur in different connections as he moves along, in a way that makes one think of the spiral tunnels whereby trains in Switzerland and Western Canada gain height. The trains emerge almost directly above where they went in, but much higher up; and similarly the reappearances of Boston's points, slightly reangled and newly illustrated as they usually are, raise our understanding of them higher each time we meet them. First to last, Boston gives us masterful teaching, with what Americans describe as 'review' and Brits call 'revision' built in.

But that is not all that Boston aims to do. Teaching is the means to his end, rather than the end itself. His goal, like that of every other real preacher, is to change those he addresses, or at least to see them changed by the power of God. Here, along with his permanent purpose of leading the unconverted to faith and the new birth, his clear purpose is to discipline Christ's disciples in reverent, realistic, hope-filled humility, as they face up to the inescapable imperfections of life in general and their own lives in particular. He wants us to be utterly sure of the wisdom and goodness of God's Providence as we adjust to the disappointments, deprivations and limitations of our lives, and to glorify God by the way we cope with them. He is consciously ministering to the many who he knows are not strong at this point, seeking to establish them in humble, prayerful steadiness. His book is preaching on paper, and if it left its readers unmoved and unchanged he would certainly count it a failure – a crook in his own lot, we might say.

IV

That brings us to my second question. Has this book a message for today? The answer, I believe, is yes, most certainly; but it is a message that moderns are likely to find very hard to hear. Why? Let me explain.

Psychologists and philosophers have noticed that it is common for people to have in their minds incompatible lines of thought, desire, valuation, expectation and purpose, and to be unaware of the incompatibility. They call this condition cognitive dissonance. Pastorally, the insight is important, for the mixture of faith and unbelief, wisdom and foolishness, spiritual discernment and spiritual myopia, that we find in all believers in this world, virtually guarantees that there will be *cognitive dissonance* in Christian minds – self-contradiction and incoherence, that is – over and over again with regard to the things of God. So it proves to be, and pastors are constantly having to detect and correct mistakes of this kind.

Now, one particular form of cognitive dissonance that is widespread today among evangelical Protestants (interestingly, you do not find it among Roman Catholics and Orthodox) is as follows. Nobody questions that Christ tells His followers to deny themselves – that is, to give to God all the personal hopes and dreams they have cherished, and accept that non-fulfilment of these may be part of His plan – and to take up their cross – that is, be willing to become discredited outcasts, like the condemned men whose ranks Jesus was to join who were made to carry the means of their crucifixion to the place appointed for it. This is a clear, sober warning from our Lord that discipleship will have its downs as well as its ups, its distresses as well as its delights, and no Christian challenges it. But at the same time the comfort-oriented materialism of our age urges that painless, trouble-free living is virtually a human right, and against this background many who believe they believe let themselves think that because they are God's children they will always be shielded from major troubles, such as strike other people, and will be led through life on a pain-free path, with all pleasant things provided, as would happen on a cruise. The brash and simplistic expression of this syndrome is found in the health and wealth gospel of some televangelists; the more reflective and sophisticated expression of it appears in the pained question, voiced when trauma comes – bereavement, betrayal, incurable disease, business collapse, or whatever – 'How could God let this happen to me?' and it further appears in the theological theories that say God would have stopped it if He could, but He couldn't, because His sovereignty is limited. Here we meet cognitive dissonance, anchored deep in people's hearts. The fantasy of nasty things kept at bay and only nice things meant for us here and now dies hard, and where it has not yet died Boston's realism, bracing, clarifying and stabilizing as it is, will not be received.

But be that as it may, the pure biblical wisdom of *The Crook in the Lot* is badly needed by many of us, and so I am delighted that it is being made available again in this handy form. And I hope that what I have written here will help a new generation to read it with understanding and gratitude to God. For truly, as Americans love to say, this is where it's at.

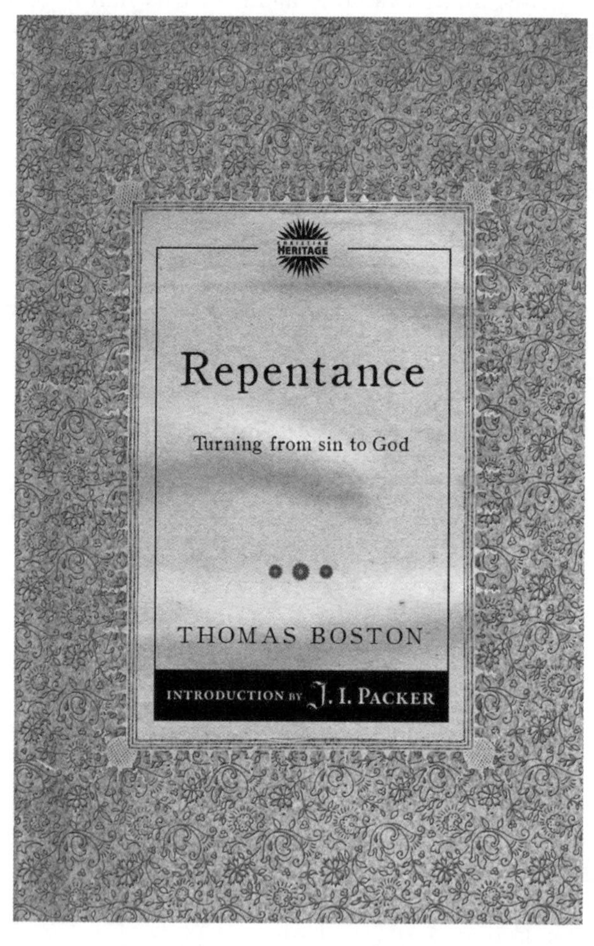

ISBN 978-1-84550-975-0

7 c

Thomas Boston

Repentance

I

The Reformation brought to light many biblical realities that had long been overlaid by mistaken ideas and thus effectively hidden from view. The true nature of the Bible's own authority, for instance, and of justification by faith and salvation by grace and of the church and the sacraments, spring to mind. Repentance also is a case in point.

In the Middle Ages, repentance was equated with 'penance'—that is, confession of sins to a priest followed by absolution and the imposing of a disciplinary penalty for the sinner to undergo in order to signalise genuine sorrow. Nor was this the end of the matter; for a distinction was drawn between eternal guilt and temporal punishment, and the theory was that while absolution remitted the former, thus saving sinners from hell, they must yet spend time in purgatory after death enduring the latter. Indulgences, however, issued at the Pope's discretion and underwritten by the treasury of the saints' superabundant merits, would secure reduction of the purgatorial period, according to the terms in which they were drafted.

It was Luther's outraged challenge to the sale of a plenary indulgence that would keep the purchaser out of purgatory no matter what his sins were, and that could be bought for persons now in purgatory as their get-out-of-jail-free card, effective immediately, which triggered the Reformation movement across Western Europe. The first two of the ninety-five theses that Luther in his dual role as university professor of Bible and preaching pastor of the Wittenberg Castle Church congregation, posted on the church door on October 31st, 1517, were as follows:

1. When our Lord and Master Jesus Christ said, 'Repent' he wanted the entire life of believers to be one of penitence.
2. This word cannot be understood as referring to penance as a sacrament (that is, confession and satisfaction [the disciplinary penalty] as administered by the ministry of priests).

Luther's positive point, that repentance means whole-hearted turning or returning to God, and that the Christian life is and must be as truly a life of repentance as a life of faith, was to find full expression in Calvin's *Institutes* (III.I, ii-iv), in the weekly set services of the Anglican Prayer Book, in a classic sermon by John Bradford the martyr, in a widely read small book by the Elizabethan Reformed and devotional theologian William Perkins, and in many Puritan utterances after that, crowned perhaps by the declaration of Philip Henry, father of Matthew, that he hoped to carry his repentance up to the gates of heaven itself. As, however, Puritan attention focused increasingly on conversion and regeneration, Puritan emphasis was more and more laid on the initial repentance leading to the penitent life, and this is reflected in the *Westminster Confession's* chapter XV, 'Of Repentance unto Life.'

1. Repentance unto life is an evangelical grace, the doctrine whereof is to be preached by every minister of the Gospel, as well as that of faith in Christ.

2. By it, a sinner, out of the sight and sense not only of the danger, but also of the filthiness and odiousness of his sins, as contrary to the holy nature, and righteous law of God; and upon the apprehension of his mercy in Christ to such as are penitent, so grieves for and hates his sins, as to turn from them unto God, purposing and endeavouring to walk with him in all the ways of his commandments.

5. Men ought not to content themselves with a general repentance, but it is every man's duty to endeavour to repent of his particular sins, particularly.

In the book now before us, Thomas Boston (1676–1732), minister of Ettrick in south Scotland, inheritor and champion of Puritan theology and of the Reformational rethinking that preceded it, links together expositions first written for his pulpit on the necessity, nature and urgency of repentance, and the folly of ignoring or postponing this life-and-death issue. The sermons have all the qualities we associate with Boston: a dazzling mastery of the text and teaching of the Bible; a profound knowledge of the human heart; great thoroughness and clarity in exposition; great skill in applicatory searching of the conscience; and a pervasive sense of the wonder and glory of God's grace in Christ to such perverse sinners as ourselves. Proper appreciation of what we have here requires, however, some preparation of both head and heart, to take us into the world of Boston's wisdom, and I propose now to say something about that.

II

Flanking a main gate into what you might call Oxford's Mecca, an area containing the Clarendon Building, the University's administrative centre; the Sheldonian Theatre, where degrees are conferred; the medieval Divinity School, and the world-famous Bodleian Library; pillars support sculptured heads of some of mankind's Big Brains. They are restored now, but when I was an undergraduate they had been weathered featureless and all you could tell as you looked at them was that they were meant to be human heads and not anything else. It is like that with the Bible-based, Puritan-ripened convictions about God and ourselves out of which Boston expounds and applies his texts. Modern thought has so weathered this faith that at first it seems to us a far-off and somewhat fuzzy historical oddity, not relevant for us at all.

Thus, Boston believes that the triune God, through whom we exist, in whose hands we are, and who will one day deal out our destiny, is *holy* in such a sense as to induce a sense of guilt and shame, unrighteousness and uncleanness, perversity and pollution, demerit and defilement, in all who realise His reality; and moreover is *sovereign* over everything in His world, even the free choices of human beings. But most today, while still acknowledging 'the one above' (or perhaps 'the man upstairs'), assume that God's nature is simply one of kindness without standards or expectations, and helpfulness that should shield everyone from harm all the time; or else they see him as an impersonal cosmic force, not *he* but *it*, making no difference to anyone, so that it is only common sense to live as if God did not exist.

Again, Boston believes that Jesus Christ, divine-human Lord and Mediator, our prophet, priest and king, crucified, risen, reigning and returning, offers Himself in the gospel to everyone, inviting and commanding all who hear to receive and trust Him as their Saviour, Master and Friend, through whom they may find forgiveness, acceptance and adoption into God's family, there to be transformed into the image of God's Son. Also, Boston believes that Jesus will one day be everyone's judge, and that everyone's destiny is either eternal heaven with Jesus or eternal hell without Him. But most today think of Jesus as one more good man who taught and modelled decent behaviour, and they dismiss whatever most Christians believe about Him as mere superstitious fancy. As for death, they conceive it as leading to either immediate happiness or immediate extinction, without Jesus being involved either way.

Again, Boston believes that the Bible is like a great illuminated circle, at the centre of which we stand with light shining on us from biblical teaching, narratives, biographies and circumstances to show us ourselves as we really are, and as God sees us, here and now; and he further believes that the Holy Spirit of God leads us to pass on ourselves the judgment that God passes, and to labour to change our ways accordingly—which is precisely what in Scripture *repentance* means. Thus, and only thus, to Boston's mind, do we learn what Paul meant when he said that all Scripture, being God-breathed, is 'profitable for teaching, for reproof, for correction, and for training in righteousness' (2 Tim. 3:16). But most today think of the Bible as at best a collection of ancient ideas about religion, some of which can still inspire but most of which are freaky and outdated, and all of which need to be relativised, in our world of multiple cultures, both religious and secular, to whatever the consensus of the culture currently surrounding us happens to be. For reason is in the saddle, shaping religion, which it sees as essentially a human construct, and while reason thus rides and drives, biblical revelation is left behind in the ditch.

And finally, Boston believes that regeneration of heart by the Holy Spirit of God imparts a truly new-created life, of which the exercise of faith in Christ, the practice of repentance toward God, the humbling of one's heart, the upsurging of joy in the Lord and the overflow of active love to God in worshipful communion and to fellow-humans in self-denying service, along with passion to progress in all of this, are the direct expressions. But most today see religion as simply a crutch and a comfort for the struggling self, something that most of us can get on well without, and so the evangelical existence just described is dismissed as surely self-deceived and hypocritical.

The world of spiritual reality in which Boston's teaching about repentance is anchored is now before us, in outline at any rate, and it has to be said at once that unless we ourselves are inhabitants of that world, or at least are prepared to discover that we should be, we shall not appreciate him as the perceptive, profound, skilful, Spirit-taught physician of the soul that in fact he is. In his own day he was admired not simply as an accomplished biblical scholar, though he was all of that, but principally as a master pastor, whose *Fourfold State* circulated throughout Scotland as the ordinary person's *vade-mecum* on the path to heaven. Today, three centuries later, this man of God yet speaks to us in print, shining the searchlight of Scripture on our disordered lives and pleading with us to face and listen to God as He speaks to us through His servant on the various matters that Boston dealt with—here, the reality or otherwise of our 'repentance unto life.' Too businesslike to aim at elegance, Boston nonetheless achieves eloquence by his down-to-earth clarity of style, expository order and skill in clinching each point by appropriate words from his Bible. And, as with some cheeses, you will find that the more you chew what He gives us, the stronger the flavour you get.

III

What sort of people do these sermons on repentance address? In a broad and basic sense, of course, like all Reformational,

Puritan and authentic Evangelical sermons, they are declarations of truth about God that are truly messages for everybody. Everyone needs to be reminded, and believers love to be reminded, over and over again, of the reality of God's holiness, awesomeness, graciousness, faithfulness, justice, greatness and glory, and these themes must ever be primary and foundational in preaching, as in Boston they invariably are. In all his sermons, God—God omnipotent, omniscient, and omnipresent; God in Christ exercising both mercy and judgment; God who searches hearts and whose wheels grind slowly but grind exceedingly small—is, so to speak, the subject and human beings the predicate; Boston is God-centred, even, as is said of Jonathan Edwards, God-intoxicated, and his first concern as a preacher is that all of us at the receiving end should be the same. We today are so used to man-centred sermons, in which God appears only as does Jeeves in P. G. Wodehouse's farcical novels, to get people out of trouble, that for some of us adjusting to Boston's perspective is a major effort. But sermons, as such, are utterances on God's behalf to stop people sinning and bring them closer to God, so it is still proper to ask: who in particular are the people whom Boston is addressing?

There is no doubt as to how our question should be answered. Boston is reaching out to impenitent religious people, old and young, high and low, of two kinds: the self-satisfied and presumptuous, and the procrastinators, whom Boston describes as the slothful and pictures as spiritual sleepers. He seeks to explode the pride of the former and the apathy of the latter, and to lead both into the repentance that both need—'salvation-work', as he calls it. So first he explains that repentance is a matter of the heart, a lifetime's task, a gift of God's Spirit through God's Word, a change involving conviction, distress, faith in Christ, humiliation of heart, 'holy shame' and violent self-dislike, a confessing, renouncing, and turning from all one's sins as one knows them and a sincere, whole-hearted turning to God in total commitment to obedience henceforth and for ever. Then he deploys as motives to repentance the command and call of God, the killing effect of sin, the prospect of death and judgment, the agony of Christ, and the dishonour that sin does to God. Then he shows at length how delay in repenting, for whatever reason, must ruin the soul. Then he dwells on the condemned state of the impenitent, however friendly the providences surrounding them may seem, and pleads once again for serious personal repentance on the part of everyone. Pursuing this story-line, as we may call it, he scatters incidentally a great deal of wisdom about the ways of God, as he regularly does in all his practical writing. To readers who are on his wavelength, he has much to give. But the wavelength question, I recognise, is a real one. There are many professed believers today whose sincerity and zeal are great but whose Christian reading has so far stopped short at what I would call Christian froth (of which, be it said, there is nowadays no shortage), and if Boston falls into their hands they may well be tempted after the first few pages to give up, feeling that this is tough stuff, old-fashioned and dry, and is doing nothing for them. Granted, Boston, like others of the sermon-publishing Puritan school, is something of an acquired taste; but to any thus stymied who turn back to this Introduction in puzzlement as to why Boston's book should be rated a classic, I say—keep going, I beg you; and have a ballpoint handy, to jot down Boston's headings as you come to them; and take note of everything he tells you about God; and when you have struggled to the end, go back and read the book again; and I guarantee that you will realise you have not been wasting your time.

Before me, as I write, is a leaflet announcing a conference retreat under the title: 'Repentance as the Way to a Blessed Life in the 21st Century.' The title declares a truth, and Boston can lead us into that blessed life as sure-footedly as anyone. So read well, think and pray about what you read, and God bless you through the perennial wisdom that His servant unfolds.

Part 3:

Two Puritan Paragons:

William Perkins
Richard Baxter

Two Puritan Paragons

I round off this set of Puritan profiles with two close-ups – portraits of a pair who, to my mind, are the outstanding figures of early and mid-period Puritanism respectively. Years ago I wrote a book on Puritanism which I titled *Among God's Giants*. In America it was re-titled *A Quest for Godliness,* which shifted its emphasis a little. My title reflected my sense of the stature of Puritanism's leaders as a company of wise and devoted pastoral pioneers. William Perkins and Richard Baxter, along with John Owen and John Bunyan, seem to me to stand out as giants among the giants, Perkins as an early Puritan, Baxter as a mid-period Puritan, and Owen and Bunyan as later Puritans. I hope that what I offer now on the first two of these will lead my readers to appreciate their outstanding qualities and join me in thanking God for them and drawing wisdom from them.

William Perkins (1558-1602)

A Puritan Pioneer

The name of William Perkins is hardly known today outside a small circle of professional historians and theologians. It may therefore come as a surprise to learn that during the half-century from 1585 to 1635 Perkins was far and away the best-known and best-selling English writer of Christian books for ordinary people. More than that, he was the best-known English international theologian, being classed with Calvin and Beza as third in what someone called 'the trinity of the orthodox'. But so indeed he was. It is a fact that almost ninety editions of works by him were published in translation in the Netherlands, fifty plus in both Switzerland and Germany, and smaller printings in half a dozen other languages. No Puritan author save Richard Baxter ever sold better than Perkins, and no Puritan thinker ever did more to shape and solidify historic Puritanism itself.

Many nowadays know that the real Puritanism was not the eccentric and combative Protestant Pharisaism that nineteenth-century novels and history books imagined. Many know that the real Puritanism was an evangelical holiness movement seeking to implement its vision of spiritual renewal, national and personal, in the church, the state and the home; in education, evangelism, and economics; in individual discipleship and devotion, and in pastoral care and competence. Many know that real Puritan piety centred upon regeneration and repentance, self-suspicion and self-examination, rational Biblicism and righteous behaviour, discursive meditation and rhetorical prayer, faith in and love to Jesus Christ as Saviour and Lord, recognition of the sovereignty of God in providence, grace, and judgment, the comfort and joy of a well-grounded assurance, the need to educate and cherish one's conscience, the spiritual war against the world, the flesh, and the devil, the ethic of discipline and duty, and the saints' hope of glory. Few however know as yet that it was Perkins, quite specifically, who established Puritanism in this mould.

Who was this man William Perkins? He is a somewhat shadowy figure, but the main facts of his life are not in doubt. He was an Elizabethan in a very precise sense, for he was born in 1558, the year in which Elizabeth became queen, and he died of unrelieved gallstones at the age of forty-four, in 1602, shortly before Elizabeth's death in 1603. He was a Warwickshire man who in 1577, aged nineteen – late in the day, by Elizabethan standards – went up to Christ's College, Cambridge, the most Puritan-minded house in the University at that time, where Laurence Chaderton, a well-known gospel preacher, later to be master of Emmanuel and Perkins's lifelong friend, became his tutor. At first Perkins ran wild, but then was converted (details not known); a passion for theology now replaced the devotion to astrological studies that had marked him hitherto, and he impressed his peers by the thoroughness and speed with which he mastered the things of God. In 1584, having graduated M.A., he was elected to a fellowship at Christ's, where he began to excel as a tutor of undergraduates. Before the year was out, following a few months of strikingly effective evangelism on a volunteer basis in Cambridge jail, he was also installed as lecturer (that is, endowed preacher) at Great St Andrews, a poor and needy parish that brought in to its vicar the less than princely stipend of 10 pounds per annum. Perkins as lecturer was not the vicar, and whatever he received for his preaching would have come from private sources. We learn that when in 1595 he left Christ's, a celibate community, to marry a lady named Timothye Cradock of Grantchester, parishioners and wealthy supporters augmented his income to ensure that his ministry at St Andrews would continue; which it did, till Perkins died seven years and seven children later. When Thomas Goodwin, twelve years old and not yet a Christian, matriculated in 1613, so he tells us, 'the Town was then filled with the discourse of the Power of Mr Perkins, his Ministry still fresh in Men's Memories,' even though Perkins had been more than ten years in his grave.

Nor was this the whole story, or even the main part of it. During the years that Perkins preached his pen was busy and he left behind him almost fifty separate treatises of various kinds, covering the whole range of theology, spirituality and ethics, and including several major pieces of biblical exposition. Perkins's special strength both in preaching and on paper was to be systematic, scholarly, solid and simple at the same time. No one else in world Protestantism had hitherto produced material of Perkins's type and range, at Perkins's level of lucidity and soon Perkins's books were appearing in French, Dutch, Italian, Spanish, Czech, German, Hungarian, Latin and Welsh. Ian Breward, writer of the best survey of Perkins's work to have appeared so far, explains Perkins's international popularity and influence as 'due to an attractive and practical piety, ability to popularise and an extraordinarily wide range of theological activity,' and observes that 'translating and publishing Perkins was a minor industry,' listing twenty-nine translators and twenty-eight publishers outside England to prove his point.[1]

'After his death,' writes William Haller, 'his disciples ... gathered up for publication or republication three tall volumes of his polemics, treatises and sermons ... No books, it is fair to say, were more often to be found upon the shelves of succeeding

1 Intro. and ed., Ian Breward, *The Work of William Perkins* (Abingdon: Sutton Courtenay Press, 1969), xi, p. 130.

generations of preachers, and the name of no preacher recurs more often in later Puritan literature. "As for his books," Fuller observed half a century later, "it is a miracle almost to conceive how thick they lye".'[2]

It was these books that determined seventeenth-century Puritanism's profile and priorities and that led the Dutch theologian Voetius in his treatise *Concerning Practical Theology*, in which many Puritan pietists are commended, to call Perkins 'the Homer [that is, the magisterial classic], of practical Englishmen.'[3]

We speak of George Stephenson as the Father of Railways because in designing the Rocket and in laying out first the Stockton and Darlington and then the Liverpool and Manchester lines he got everything basically right, albeit at a rudimentary level, so that the development of steam traction world-wide could and did proceed most successfully by following the guidelines he had established. In the same way we should call William Perkins the Father of Puritanism, for it was he more than anyone else who crystallised and delimited the essence of mainstream Puritan Christianity for the next hundred years. This makes it ironical, first, that Perkins detested and refused the word 'Puritan' as a label for himself and those like him and, second that among the forty or so Puritan writers who have been reprinted for the common Christian reader during the past forty years Perkins's name has hardly appeared. Banner of Truth republished *The Art of Prophesying* (i.e. *Preaching*) in 1996, and Ian Breward excerpted a selection for scholars from Perkins's books (*The Work of William Perkins*; Sutton Courtenay Press, 1970), and that is all. To be sure, the irony diminishes on closer inspection, for the word 'Puritan' in Perkins's day carried implications of both a revolutionary spirit and a separatist

2 William Haller, *The Rise of Puritanism* (New York: Columbia University Press, 1938), p. 65; quoting Thomas Fuller, *Abel Redevivus*, 1651, p. 434.

3 Tr. and ed. J.W. Beardslee, *Reformed Dogmatics* (New York: Oxford University Press, 1966), pp. 274-5.

purpose, and Perkins's plain-glass treatments of basic themes were all superseded by later Puritan presentations that were fuller and had more punch. But the key fact remains as stated: Perkins was the pioneer who shaped Puritanism in a decisive way, imparting to it the qualities that were to characterise it for the next hundred years.

Before Perkins, Calvinistic Anglicans seeking change in the national church had not been at one on their goals and priorities, and a strident hotheadedness had marked their public style. Some had sought Prayer Book revision, so as to get further away from Roman-type worship, and had flaunted their nonconformity to the established liturgical order. Some had sought a workable pattern of parochial church discipline, and had flung themselves into the crypto-Presbyterian classism movement, which had this as one of its aims. Not many had yet focused their goal in evangelistic terms, as the conversion of England to real godliness through teaching, preaching and pastoral care. Perkins's example and influence, however, along with that of parish clergymen like Richard Greenham and Richard Rogers, Arthur Hildersam and John Dod, established mainstream Puritanism as a movement majoring on evangelism and spiritual life, bearing with ecclesiastical inconvenience for the time being in order to fulfil in the Church of England a full-scale soul-saving ministry. Puritanism, with its complex of biblical, devotional, ecclesiastical, reformational, polemical and cultural concerns, came of age, we might say, with Perkins, and began to display characteristically a wholeness of spiritual vision and a maturity of Christian patience that had not been seen in it before.

Perkins's Ministry

How, we may now ask, did Perkins himself approach his own ministerial work? We are told that in daily life he was a man of peace, studied moderation, and a personal sanctity that impressed everyone. He was faithful in fulfilling his role as a professional academic and a college tutor, but it is clear that his wider ministry at Great St Andrews, and the popular writing that went with it, were his chief concerns. We are told that at the head of the title-page of each of his manuscripts he would write this message to himself: 'Thou art a Minister of the Word: Mind thy business.' That, certainly, is what he did.

Here is Benjamin Brook's account of Perkins as a preacher. It goes back to Thomas Fuller, who though a royalist in politics was a Puritan in his Christianity, and was fascinated by Perkins, who died six years before he was born; Fuller researched Perkins, wrote a brief life of him, and introduced him as a model of faithfulness in ministry in several of his own writings. Drawing on Fuller, Brook pinpoints Perkins's pulpit strengths as follows:

> His hearers consisted of collegians, townsmen and people from the country. This required those peculiar ministerial endowments which providence had richly bestowed upon him. In all his discourses, his style and his subject were accommodated to the capacities of the common people, while, at the same time, the pious scholars heard him with admiration ... Mr Perkins's sermons were *all law* and *all gospel*. He was a rare instance of those opposite gifts meeting in so eminent a degree in the same preacher, even the vehemence and thunder of Boanerges, to awaken sinners to a sense of their sin and danger, and to drive them from destruction; and the persuasion and comfort of Barnabas, to pour the wine and oil of gospel consolation into their wounded spirits. He used to apply the terrors of the law so directly to the consciences of his hearers, that their hearts would often sink under the convictions; and he used to pronounce the word damn with so peculiar an emphasis, that it left a doleful echo in their ears a long time after.[4]

His preaching was as erudite and edifying as it was authoritative and clear. 'In a word,' declares Fuller, 'the Scholar could have no learneder, the Townsmen no plainer Sermons.' And again: 'Our Perkins brought the schools into the Pulpit, and unshelling their controversies out of their hard school-terms, made thereof plain and wholesome meat for his people.'[5]

---

4 Benjamin Brook, *The Lives of the Puritans*, (1813, repr. Pittsburgh: Soli Deo Gloria, 1994), II. p. 130.

5 Thomas Fuller, *The Holy State*, (1642), p. 89.

Majestic and magisterial, expository and evangelical, informal and applicatory, Perkins's preaching set standards for the whole Puritan movement thereafter, just as it brought benefit to great numbers in the Cambridge of his own day.

But this was not the whole of his ministry. Like his older contemporary, Richard Greenham of Dry Drayton, just outside Cambridge, Perkins became known as an expert in spiritual pathology, and he fulfilled a notable counselling ministry to confused and tormented souls who for one reason or another feared themselves spiritually ruined and lost. Here is one example from Perkins's gaol ministry of 1584, narrated by Samuel Clarke in a book dated 1654. A young felon mounting the scaffold looked panicky and half-dead. Perkins, attending the execution as chaplain,

> laboured to cheer up his spirits, and finding him still in agony, and distress of mind, he said to him, What man? What is the matter with thee? Art thou afraid of death?
>
> Ah no (said the prisoner, shaking his head) but of a worser thing.
>
> Sayest thou so (said Master Perkins) come down again man, and thou shalt see what God's grace will do to strengthen thee: Whereupon the prisoner coming down, Master Perkins took him by the hand and made him kneel down with himself at the ladder foot ... when that blessed man of God made such an effectual prayer in confession of sins ... as made the prisoner burst out into abundance of tears; and Master Perkins finding that he had brought him low enough, even to hell gates, he proceeded to the second part of his prayer, and therein to show him the Lord Jesus ... stretching forth his blessed hand of mercy ... which he did so sweetly press with such heavenly art ... as made him break into new showers of tears for joy of the inward consolation which he found ... who (the prayer being ended) rose from his knees cheerfully, and went up the ladder again so comforted, and took his death with such patience, and alacrity, as if he actually saw himself delivered from the hell which he feared before, and heaven opened for the receiving of his soul.[6]

---

6 Samuel Clarke, *The Marrow of Ecclesiastical History*, (1654), pp. 416-17; quoted from Breward, op cit., 9-10, with modernised spelling.

Nor was it only to persons of the criminal class that Perkins ministered in this way. It is well known that at the end of the sixteenth century many serious souls were troubled and often desperate about their condition and prospects before God, and this is sometimes seen as the unhealthy fruit of injudicious and excessive Puritan preaching about predestination and hell-fire. That the Puritans were never mealy-mouthed on these two topics is certainly true, but all the evidence shows that they presented them in a pastorally responsible way and a more adequate explanation of the distresses people felt centres upon four other factors.

First, uncertainties and anxieties about the future pervaded late Elizabethan community life, partly as a reaction to what seemed to be the permanent embattled hostility to England of the whole Roman Catholic world, partly at least as a spinoff from the enterprising but often anarchic and calamitous individualism that had developed during Elizabeth's reign on the economic and political fronts; and this mood of anxiety naturally infected English religion.

Second, as in the modern West a quarter of the population needs treatment for depression at some point in their lives, so in Puritan times depressive tendencies, linked as so often today with obsessive-compulsive neuroses, were widespread; indeed, it was an era in which a measure of 'melancholy', as depression was then called, was expected and even cultivated among the cultured, so naturally problems of spiritual depression were widespread.

Third, in that age of compulsory church attendance Puritans like Perkins rightly laid stress on the need for self-suspicion and self-search in order to arouse the complacent among their hearers to the possibility of their still being unconverted and hell-bound, and such teaching has a naturally traumatic and anxious-making effect, as of course it is intended to.

And, fourth and most important of all, the Holy Spirit worked in power in England throughout the Puritan period, so that the impact of gospel preaching, conviction of sin, demands for repentance, and the fear of divine rejection, went very deep.

I venture to affirm that there was nothing intrinsically unhealthy about any of this from a spiritual standpoint; much unhealthier was, and is, the unconcern of those who refuse to care about the issues of eternity as the gospel sets them out and who ridicule preachers and people who do in fact care about them. That persons convicted of sin, and those whom we would label clinically depressed, should feel hopeless and helpless should not cause us surprise. And anyhow, the record states that many troubled souls came to Perkins one on one, and he was able to help them to faith, hope, confidence, and devoted discipleship. As Fuller quaintly puts it: 'An excellent Chirurgeon [*surgeon*] he was at jointing of a broken soul, and at stating of a doubtful conscience.'[7] In Perkins's pastoral counselling, no less than in his pulpit expositions, wisdom about the paths God opens to conversion and the peace God gives to troubled hearts flowed abundantly, and there was joy in Cambridge as a result.

The many businesslike laymen's books on principles and problems of Christian living that came from Perkins's pen were part of this same ministry. They were written, not to advance the author's reputation and career, but to build up Englishmen in the Christian faith. When Perkins's ministry began, Protestant England had no devotional literature of its own at popular level at all. Literate clergy – a minority at that stage in Anglican history, be it said – could enlarge their overall Christian understanding by reading Calvin, his successor at Geneva, Beza, the *Decades* of Bullinger, and the two official Anglican books of Homilies. If questions of church order captured their interest, they could pursue them via the keen though dryish writings of Cartwright, Whitgift, and Travers. If they wanted anti-Roman reinforcing, Jewel's *Apology* and Foxe's *Acts and Monuments* were available. But there was nothing whatever as yet for their literate parishioners to read, to build them up in the faith.

7 Thomas Fuller, *The Holy State*, p. 90.

Perkins set himself to fill this gap. If you think of him as in this respect a forerunner of J.C. Ryle, C.S. Lewis, and John Stott, you will not be far wrong. Perkins devoted his first-class mind and his flair for simple forceful statement to the production of popular nurturing literature for laypeople. Let us now survey his achievement.

The Apostles' Creed, the Lord's Prayer, and the Ten Commandments were, and are, the three classic formulations on which mainstream Christianity rests, and around which the Prayer Book Catechism and countless other sixteenth- and seventeenth-century catechisms were constructed. Perkins composed expositions of all three: *An Exposition of the Symbol, or Creed of the Apostles* (1595); *An Exposition of the Lord's Prayer* (1592) and chapters 19-29 of *A Golden Chain: or, The Description of Theology* (1590 in Latin, 1591 in English), where the Decalogue is systematically laid open. Starting with the dictum, 'Theology is the science of living blessedly for ever,' this latter work analyses all God's purposes and procedures in relation to human destiny. It sold well, running through nine editions in thirty years. In addition, Perkins composed *The Foundation of Christian Religion, Gathered into Six Principles: And it is to be Learned of Ignorant People, that they may be fit to hear Sermons with Profit, and to Receive the Lord's Supper with Comfort* (1590). This was a question-and-answer evangelistic catechism on the contents of the gospel. Beginning with an address to the ignorant, listing thirty-two 'common opinions' in which their ignorance found expression, it showed them in simplest form (1) God's triunity; (2) man's sin and lostness; (3) Christ's saving work; (4) the individual's salvation 'by faith alone apprehending and applying Christ with all his merits to himself';[8] (5) the means to faith, namely the Word preached, backed by sacraments and prayer; and (6) the prospect of heaven for the godly and hell for unbelievers. In writing this work, Perkins became the spiritual

8 *The Workes of that Famous and Worthy Minister of Christ in the Universitie of Cambridge Mr William Perkins*, (1616), I. pp. 32-69.

ancestor of moderns like Michael Green and Nicky Gumbel, and alerts us today, four centuries after, to the need for initial knowledge of the Christian ABC if one is to get the best out of expository preaching. These pieces by Perkins were the first significant resources for the Puritan discipling of England, and the catechism in particular was very widely used for half a century after its composer's death.[9]

Producing these basic items was only, however, a small part of Perkins's labour as a formulator and populariser of Puritan faith and practice. Consider the following series of books (all fairly small, despite their titular fulsomeness), which Perkins wrote with a lay readership directly in view.

1. *A Treatise Tending unto a Declaration whether a Man be in the Estate of Damnation, or in the Estate of Grace; and if he be in the first, how he may in time come out of it; if in the second, how he may discern it, and persevere in the same to the end* (1588). Described by Perkins himself as 'a Dialogue of the State of a Christian Man Gathered Here and There Out of the Sweet and Savoury Writings of Master Tyndale and Master Bradford' [William Tyndale the Bible translator and John Bradford the Marian martyr], this item, in the words of Ian Breward, 'sums up in brief form what were to become the classical concerns of puritan piety'[10] – that is, in a nutshell, saving grace, saving faith, and holy life.
2. *A Case of Conscience, the Greatest that Ever Was: How a Man may Know whether he be a child of God, or no: Resolved by the Word of God* (1592). This is an ingenious dialogue between the apostle John and his interlocutor, 'Church,' in which every verse of 1 John is presented as the answer to some error, uncertainty, or confusion about assurance of salvation that was abroad among English churchmen in the late sixteenth century.

9 Breward, p. 147.

10 Breward, p. 355.

3. *A Grain of Mustard Seed: Or, The Least Measure of Grace that is or can be Effectual to Salvation* (1597). Viewing conversion as a life-process which the Holy Spirit works in sinners by stages once he has united them to Christ, Perkins here argues that the desire for full conversion, that is, for strong faith in Christ and thorough repentance, is itself a sign that one is already accepted by God, even though faith and repentance have hardly begun to appear in one's actual performance.

4. *Two Treatises: 1. Of the nature and practice of Repentance. 2. Of the combat of the flesh and spirit* (1593). For the Puritans, as for the Reformers, repentance was a fruit of faith and a life-long discipline of the Christian life. Perkins's presentation is a searching analysis of what repentance involves. In his preface to it he affirms his solidarity with Protestants who preceded him as follows:

    And whereas these have been published heretofore in English two sermons of repentance, one by Mr Bradford Martyr, the other by Mr Arthur Dent; sermons indeed which have done much good: my meaning [intention] is not to add thereunto, or to teach another doctrine, but only renew and revive the memory of that which they have taught.

    Neither let it trouble thee that the principal divines of this age, whom in this treatise I follow, may seem to be at difference in treating of repentance. For some make it a fruit of faith, containing two parts, mortification and vivification: some make faith a part of it, by dividing contrition, faith, new obedience [*marginal reference to Melanchthon*]: some make it all one with regeneration [*marginal reference to Calvin, who also proposed the mortification-vivification analysis*]. The difference is not in the substance of doctrine, but in the logical manner of handling it ... repentance ... is taken two ways ... Generally for the whole conversion of the sinner, and so it may contain contrition, faith, new obedience ... and be confounded with regeneration. It is taken particularly

> for the renovation of life and behaviour: and so it is a fruit of faith. And this only sense do I follow in this treatise. [11]

The treatise on repentance includes an elaborate scheme for self-examination by the light of the Decalogue and the gospel, and both treatises hit out hard at the Tridentine teaching on meritorious human acts.

5. *How to Live, and that Well, in all Estates and Times, Specially, When Helps and Comforts fail* (1601). This is an extended sermon on Habakkuk 2:4, showing how Bible-based faith brings peace, joy, godliness and good hope.
6. *A Salve for a Sick Man: or, a Treatise containing the Nature, Differences, and Kinds of Death: As also the Right Manner of Dying Well. And it may serve for Spiritual Instruction to 1. Mariners when they go to sea; 2. Soldiers when they go to battle; 3. Women when they travail with child* (1595). That preparation for dying is a duty and discipline of the Christian life may sound strange in modern Christian ears, but the Reformers, Puritans, and earlier evangelicals, like the mediaevals, were clear about it, and Perkins handles the theme in a forthright gospel-based and down-to-earth way, which since death is the one certain fact of life seems entirely appropriate.
7. *The Whole Treatise of the Cases of Conscience ... Taught and Delivered by Mr W Perkins in his holyday Lectures* [= Sunday sermons], *examined by his own briefs* [manuscripts], *and published for the common good by T Pickering* (1606). This posthumous publication was the pioneer attempt to work out a full-scale Protestant casuistry for the moral guidance

11 Workes, I.454; spelling modernised, as in all quotations from Perkins's text. The treatise runs from pp. 453-74. Bradford's sermon is in *Works of John Bradford: Sermons and Treatises*, (Cambridge: Parker Society, 1848, repr. Edinburgh: Banner of Truth, 1988), pp. 20-81. The sermon by Arthur Dent, author of *The Plain Man's Pathway to Heaven* (1601), one of the two books that formed the dowry of Mrs John Bunyan, has not been reprinted.

> of all God's people. Starting from the assertion that there is 'a certain and infallible doctrine, propounded and taught in the Scriptures, whereby the consciences of men distressed, may be quieted and relieved,'[12] the treatise deals in order with three sets of questions: first, those relating to personal salvation, assurance, and various forms of spiritual distress; second, those relating to the knowledge and worship of God; and third, those relating to the practice of Christian virtues (prudence, clemency, temperance, liberality, justice is Perkins's list) in the family, the church and the commonwealth.

These seven items, taken together, point us to the concerns that were central in Perkins's ministry. As a professional theologian of the Church of England, he used his gifts of lucid analysis and straightforward exposition to fill gaps in the Church's pastoral resources as he saw them, and so to provide Englishmen, both from the pulpit and on paper, with guidance on godliness from the cradle of conversion to the grave. The guidance he gave was Bible-based, according to the principles of literal and contextual interpretation established by the Reformers; it was Calvinistic, in the second-generation Aristotelian manner of Beza, Calvin's successor at Geneva for forty years, and of Zanchius, the converted Italian Thomist, with his colleagues Ursinus and Olevianus, who taught and wrote Reformed theology at Heidelberg; it was practical, being attuned at every point to the business of finding and following the path of eternal life; and it was experiential, in the sense that it focused constantly on motives, desires, distresses, graces and disgraces in the heart and inner life, as the source from which both obedience to God and its opposite take their rise.

Perkins gave prime attention throughout his ministry to the religious concerns already indicated – each person's need of regeneration; the quest for the peace and joy of assurance; the duty and discipline of self-examination to uncover one's

12 Workes, III. 1f. (1613). The Treatise occupies pp. 1-152.

sins, and of invoking Christ constantly by faith to cover them by His blood; the experience of flesh-spirit conflict; the reality of falls and recoveries as one travels the path of obedience; battles against doubts, discouragements and depression; the practice of lifelong repentance, and conscientious avoidance of wrongdoing. By concentrating on these things Perkins earned from the German writer August Lang the description, 'father of pietism', inasmuch as reading Perkins's practical works sparked and fed the continental movement, particularly in Holland and Germany, that went by this name. Pietism, so-called, was a seventeenth and eighteenth century development within Protestant state churches and Europe-wide Roman Catholicism. It was a renewing of personal devotion, marked by the principles, practices and priorities, the attitudes and aspirations, that were mentioned above. We should at once note here that the anti-intellectual, anti-cultural, anti-national-church attitudes, plus the emotionalistic and legalistic and individualistic inclinations, that marked and marred some later pietists represent deviations from, and indeed contradictions of, Perkins's Puritan humanism. With that (admittedly, rather heavy!) qualification, however, we should accept 'father of pietism'[13] as a true label for Perkins, and treat the phrase as a title of honour. The first note in any definition of pietism, after all, is that it gives priority to piety. Perkins did this, insistently and robustly; and so, I venture to say, should we all.

Precepts for Spiritual Progress

In *A Grain of Mustard Seed* Perkins depicted the sinner's conversion through the Holy Spirit as typically a complex unitary process involving the whole person over a period of time, and he urged that the only final proof that it has started is that it advances – in other words, that the personal change from natural sinfulness to supernatural godliness continues. At the end of the

13 A. Lang, *Puritanismus und Pietismus*, (Neukirchen Kreis Moers, 1941), pp. 126-31; reference taken from Breward, p. 131.

book he speaks his mind on the way to ensure growth in grace, in a passage so striking that I cite it at length and claim for it classic status in the literature of Western spirituality. Here, then, is Perkins explaining his assertion that 'the ... beginnings of grace are counterfeit unless they increase', and showing us as he does what for him constitutes health in the Christian's inner life.

> The wickedness of man's nature and the depth of hypocrisy is such that a man may and can easily transform himself into the counterfeit and resemblance of any grace of God. Therefore I put down in this last conclusion a certain note whereby the gifts of God may be discerned, namely that they grow up and increase as a grain of mustard seed to a great tree and bear fruit answerably. The grace in the heart is like to the grain of mustard seed in two things: first, it is small to see at the beginning; secondly, after it is cast into the ground of the heart, it increaseth speedily and spreadeth itself. Therefore, if a man at the first have but some little feeling of his wants, some weak and faint desire, some small obedience, he must not let this spark of grace go out, but these motions of the Spirit must be increased by the use of the word, sacraments and prayer; and they must daily be stirred up by meditating, endeavouring, striving, asking, seeking, knocking (Matt. 25:26; 2 Tim. 1:6). As for such motions of the heart that last for a week or a month and after vanish away, they are not to be regarded. And the Lord by the prophet Hosea complains of them saying, O Ephraim, thy righteousness is like the morning dew (Hosea 6:4).
>
> Therefore, considering grace unless it be confirmed and exercised is indeed no grace, I will here add certain rules of direction that the more easily we may put in practice the spiritual exercises of invocation, faith and repentance, and thereby also quicken the seeds and beginnings of grace.
>
> 1. In what place soever thou art, whether alone or abroad, by day or by night, and whatsoever thou art doing, set thyself in the presence of God. Let this persuasion always take place in thy heart, that thou art before the living God: and do thy endeavour that this persuasion may smite thy heart

with awe and reverence and make thee afraid to sin. This counsel the Lord gave Abraham (Gen. 17:1). This thing was also practised by Enoch who for this cause is said to walk with God.

2. Esteem of every present day as the day of thy death: and therefore live as though thou wert dying and do those good duties every day that thou wouldest do if thou wert dying. This is Christian watchfulness; and remember it.

3. Make catalogues and bills of thine own sins, specially of those sins that have most dishonoured God and wounded thine own conscience. Set them before thee often, specially then when thou hast any particular occasion of renewing thy repentance, that thy heart by this doleful sight may be further humbled. This was David's practice when he considered his ways and turned his feet to God's commandments, and when he confessed the sins of his youth (Ps. 119:59; Ps. 25). This was Job's practice, when he said he was not able to answer one of a thousand of his sins unto God (Job 9:3).

4. When thou first openst thine eyes in a morning, pray to God and give him thanks heartily. God then shall have his honour and thy heart shall be the better for it the whole day following. For we see in experience, that vessels keep long the taste of liquour with which they were first seasoned. And when thou liest down, let that be the last also, for thou knowest not whether fallen asleep, thou shalt ever rise again alive. Good therefore it is that thou shouldest give up thyself into the hands of God, whilst thou art waking.

5. Labour to see and feel thy spiritual poverty, that is to see the want of grace in thyself, specially those inward corruptions of unbelief, pride, self-love, etc. Labour to be displeased with thyself: and labour to feel that by reason of them thou standest in need of every drop of the blood of Christ to heal and cleanse thee from these wants. And let this practice take such place with thee, that if thou be demanded what in thine estimation is the vilest of the creatures upon the earth, thine heart and conscience may

answer with a loud voice, I, even I, by reason of mine own sins: and again, if thou be demanded what is the best thing in the world for thee, thy heart and conscience may answer with a loud and strong cry, One drop of the blood of Christ to wash away my sins.

6. Shew thyself to be a member of Christ and a servant of God, not only in the general calling of a Christian, but also in the particular calling in which thou art placed. It is not enough for a magistrate to be a Christian man, but he must also be a Christian magistrate. It is not enough for a master of a family to be a Christian man, but he must also be a Christian in his family and in the trade which he followeth daily. Not everyone that is a common hearer of the word and a frequenter of the Lord's table is therefore a good Christian, unless his conversation in his private house, and in his private affairs and dealings be suitable. There is a man to be seen what he is.

7. Search the Scriptures to see what is sin and what is not sin in every action. This done, carry in thy heart a constant and resolute purpose not to sin in anything, for faith and a purpose of sinning can never stand together.

8. Let thine endeavour be suitable to thy purpose and therefore do nothing at any time against thy conscience, rightly informed by the word. Exercise thyself to eschew every sin and to obey God in every one of his commandments that pertain either to the general calling of a Christian, or to thy particular calling. This did good Josiah, who turned unto God with all his heart, according to all the law of Moses and thus did Zechariah and Elizabeth, that walked in all the commandments of God without reproof (2 Kings 23:25; Luke 1:6).

9. If at any time, against thy purpose and resolution, thou be overtaken with any sin little or great, lie not in it, but speedily recover thyself, confessing thine offence and by prayer intreat the Lord to pardon the same, and that earnestly: till such time as thou findest thy conscience truly pacified and thy care to eschew the same sin increased.

10. Consider often of the right and proper end of thy life in this world, which is not to seek profit, honour, pleasure, but that in serving of men we might serve God in our callings. God could, if it so pleased him, preserve man without the ministry of man, but his pleasure is to fulfil his work and will, in the preservation of our bodies and the salvation of our souls, by the employment of men in his service, every one according to his vocation. Neither is there so much as a bondslave, but he must in and by his faithful service to his master, serve the Lord. Men therefore do commonly profane their labours and their lives by aiming at a wrong end, when all their care consisteth only in getting sufficient maintenance for them and theirs, for the obtaining of credit, riches and carnal commodities. For thus men serve themselves, and not God or men, much less do they serve God in serving of men.

11. Give all thy diligence to make thy election sure and to gather manifold tokens thereof. For this observe the works of God's providence, love and mercy, both in thee and upon thee, from time to time: for the serious consideration of them and the laying of them together when they are many and several, minister much direction, assurance of God's favour and comfort. This was the practice of David (1 Sam. 17:34,36; Ps. 23).

12. Think evermore thy present estate, whatsoever it be, to be the best estate for thee, because whatsoever befalls thee, though it be sickness, or any other affliction or death, befalls thee of the good providence of God. That this may be better done, labour to see and acknowledge a providence of God as well in poverty as in abundance, as well in disgrace as in good report, as well in sickness as in health, as well in life as in death.

13. Pray continually, I mean not by solemn and set prayer, but by secret and inward ejaculations of the heart; that is by a continual elevation of mind unto Christ sitting at the right hand of God the Father, and that either by prayer or giving of thanks, so often as any occasion shall be offered.

14. Think often of the worst and most grievous things that may befall thee, either in this life or death, for the name of Christ. Make a reckoning of them and prepare thyself to bear them, that when they come, they may not seem strange, but be borne the more easily.

15. Make conscience of idle, vain, unhonest and ungodly thoughts, for these are the seeds and beginnings of actual sin in word and deed. This want of care in ordering and composing our thoughts is often punished with a fearful temptation in the very thought, called of divines *tentatio blasphemiarum*, a temptation of blasphemies.

16. When any good motion or affection ariseth in the heart, suffer it not to pass away, but feed it by reading, meditating, praying.

17. Whatsoever good thing thou goest about, whether it be in word or deed, do it not in conceit of thyself or in the pride of thy heart, but in humility, ascribing the power whereby thou doest thy work and the praise thereof to God. Otherwise thou shalt find by experience, God will curse thy best doings.

18. Despise not civil honesty: good conscience and good manners go together. Therefore remember to make conscience of lying and customable swearing in common talk. Contend not either in deed or word with any man, be courteous and gentle to all, good or bad. Bear with men's wants and frailties, hastiness, forwardness, self-liking, curiousness, etc., passing them by as being not perceived. Return not evil for evil, but rather good for evil. Use meat, drink and apparel in that manner and measure that they may further godliness and may be, as it were, signs in which thou mayest express the hidden grace of thy heart. Strive not to go beyond any, unless it be in good things. Go before thine equals in the giving of honour, rather than in taking of it, making conscience of thy word, and let it be as a bond. Profess no more outwardly than thou hast inwardly in heart, oppress or defraud no man in bargaining, in all companies either do good, or take good.

19. Cleave not by inordinate affection to any creature, but above all things quiet and rest thy mind in Christ; above all dignity and honour, above all cunning and policy, above all glory and honour, above all health and beauty, above all joy and delight, above all fame and praise, above all mirth and consolation that man's heart can feel or devise beside Christ.

With these rules of practice, join rules of meditation: whereof I propound six unto thee, as I find them set down by a learned divine called Victor Strigelius.

i. We must not fall away from God for any creature.
ii. Infinite eternity is far to be preferred before the short race of this mortal life.
iii. We must hold fast the promise of grace, though we lose temporal blessings, and they also in death must needs be left.
iv. Let the love of God in Christ and the love of the church for Christ be strong in thee and prevail against all other affections.
v. It is the principal art of a Christian to believe things invisible, to hope for things deferred, to love God when he shews himself to be an enemy and thus to persevere unto the end.
vi. It is a most effectual remedy for any grief to quiet ourselves in a confidence of the presence and help of God, and to ask of him, and withal to wait either for some easement or deliverance.[14]

Perkins the Theologian

Educationalist, populariser and gap-filler, rapid reader, lightning writer, and master crafter of simplicity without shallowness,

14 Breward, pp. 405-10; Workes, I. pp. 642-44. Victor Strigelius was a Lutheran divine who taught at Heidelberg. Perkins, after saying he will quote six 'rules of meditation' [guidelines for devotional reflection] from Strigelius, adds a seventh, 'All the works of God are done in contrary means,' which is apparently a way of saying that as God works out His purpose things are regularly the opposite of what they seem, as Christ's cross was victory over Satan, in the form of seeming defeat by him.

father both of pietism as a European ethos and of Puritanism as an English ideology, Perkins produced luminous didactic treatments of many subjects that I have not yet mentioned, among them the callings of Christian people; Christian family life; 'the virtue of equity, or moderation of mind'[15]; the role of the professional ministry; the principles of homiletics; the functioning of conscience; the worship of God; the control of the tongue; the errors of Rome; and the doctrine of predestination. Clearly, however, the realities of religion in the regenerate – in other words, conversion, assurance, devotion, and biblically-ordered behaviour – were always central to his interest. Kendall's statement that Perkins 'devoted himself primarily to showing men that they must, and how they can, make their calling and election sure to themselves' is too narrow;[16] Perkins's first concern was that people should be Christians, and his aim of helping them to know they were Christians came second. The passage just quoted brings together the main things he had to say about the believer's inner life, which is the touchstone of Christian reality, and this profile of the growing saint gives us a vantage-point from which to review Perkins's theology as a whole, asking as we go how each aspect of it bears on what we now see to be its author's major focus.

The shape and substance of didactic devotional writing depends always on three things: the writers' understanding of what the Bible teaches about union with Christ and discipleship to Him, their view of the spiritual needs of their envisaged readers, and their own experience of walking with God. If they have undergone adult conversion, what they write will likely highlight the contrast between life with and without God, as Paul, Augustine, Bunyan, G.K. Chesteron and C.S. Lewis illustrate. Perkins, too, is a copybook example of this, as the above extract shows.

---

15 Breward, p. 481. The title of the treatise is *Epieikeia*. It is based on Philippians 4:5.

16 R.T. Kendall, *Calvin and English Calvinism to 1649*, (Oxford: Oxford University Press, 1979), p. 54.

The real Christian life, as Perkins conceives it, is both aspirational and transformational. It is aspirational in that it centres throughout on heartfelt endeavour to exercise prayerful faith – that is, informed trust in the once-crucified, now risen Saviour and Lord Jesus Christ – and with that to practise repentance – that is, self-search for sinful behaviour and sinful habits of heart, past and present – in order with God's help to leave them behind, and so clear the ground for holiness (law-keeping in love) henceforth. The information on which faith's appeal to the Father and the Son is founded and on which faith's hope and assurance directly rest, concerns justification and adoption into God's family through Christ's reconciling cross. And the Christian life is transformational in that the change aspired to and prayed for now noticeably begins to take place. Increasingly, those who thus pray and seek a re-ordering of their lives from the inside out find their identity, contentment and peace in further pursuing their quest, while their awareness grows that they are now different persons from what they once were; for they have come to be in Christ, the Holy Spirit now indwells them, and they can be sure that God the Father loves them savingly and will continue thus loving them for ever. Later Puritans would organise this sense of new reality under the rubric of regeneration; this however is not one of Perkins's technical terms, any more than it is in the Westminster Confession and Catechisms, or in the writings of William Tyndale the Bible translator, and John Bradford, the Reformation martyr, by whom the shape of this aspirational-transformational life of grace was first spelled out.

In delineating England's spiritual needs, Perkins mentions many forms of immorality and irreligion, but clearly what troubled him most was the Protestant formalism and spiritual complacency of his own era which had replaced its earlier Roman Catholic equivalent. So his ministry tasks, as he saw them, boiled down with exact precision to afflicting the comfortable and comforting the afflicted.

Basic to all Perkins's work is a desire to maintain continuity with the Reformational heritage, both at home and abroad, and to disciple people in it. As Kendall truly states, 'he saw himself as being in the mainstream of the Church of England, which he often defended.'[17] He had no sympathy with the advocates of separation over questions of church order; as long as the Church was committed to Reformation orthodoxy and he himself was free to teach, preach, and apply that orthodoxy, his Anglican loyalty would not be in doubt, even when he had to endure harassment from within the system. (An example of this was that in 1587 he had to answer to the University Vice-Chancellor for saying in a sermon that the Prayer Book requirements of kneeling at communion and having the celebrant administer the elements to himself were not the best options.) Nonetheless, loyalty to the established system was integral to the Christianity he taught.

As for the wider Protestant heritage, it is important to see that Perkins, who identified himself as a Calvinist, absorbed the teaching not only of Calvin but of other Reformed writers also, such as, apparently, Bucer, Bullinger, Musculus, and Peter Martyr, and particularly Beza of Geneva and Zanchius of Heidelberg. A long appendix from Beza rounds off *A Golden Chain* (the basic material of which had been borrowed from Beza in the first place), and a digest of Zanchius' thoughts about assurance fills more than half of *A Case of Conscience*; and Perkins's own account of faith and assurance clearly reflects the influence of these two giants. Generically, Reformation theology conceived faith as the Christian's whole-souled reliance on the Christ of the biblical promises for a right relationship with God. Calvin had defined faith as a Spirit-taught persuasion of God's favour for Christ's sake, in other words as an assured confidence of mind and heart, and he had explained Peter's summons in 2 Peter 1:10 to 'make your calling and election sure' as a simple plea for behaviour consistent with one's Christian profession.[18] Perkins,

17 R.T. Kendall, *Calvin and English Calvinism to 1649*, (Oxford: Oxford University Press, 1979), p. 54.

18 'Now we shall possess a right definition of faith if we call it a firm and certain knowledge of God's benevolence towards us, founded on the truth of the freely given promise in Christ, both revealed to our minds and sealed in our hearts through the Holy Spirit', *Inst.* III. ii. 7.

however, extended the definition of faith to include both the will (that is, the desire and longing) to believe which precedes active trust, and the act of the soul applying the Christ of the promises to one's own troubled heart and guilty conscience; and he follows Beza and Zanchius in understanding 2 Peter 1:10 as telling Christians to make their standing 'in the life', as the Welsh phrase it, sure and certain to themselves, by noting how grace has already changed them.

Perkins linked this view of the verse with his own clearly focused Thomistic concept of conscience as the mind working its way through what he called 'practical syllogisms' for either disapproval and condemnation or approval and comfort. In a practical syllogism the major premise would be a moral or spiritual rule, ideally a biblical declaration; the minor premise would be a factual observation; and the conclusion a moral judgment. A simple example, which Perkins actually uses, as many of us also do today, is:

> Everyone that believes is the child of God;
> But I believe;
> Therefore I am the child of God.

Kendall finds Perkins's account of faith confused and his path to assurance illusory, but his criticisms seem to depend on separating the mind and the will in a way that Perkins never did, on equating biblical self-examination with introspection, and on forgetting Perkins's axiom that real grace grows, and proves its reality thereby.[19] In my opinion, Perkins was right, first to analyse conscience as operating, in however compressed a way, by practical syllogisms, and second to affirm that scriptural self-examination will ordinarily yield the Christian solid grounds for confidence as to his or her regeneration and standing with God.

Basic too to all Perkins's work was his insistence that Holy Scripture must be received as the teaching and testimony of God, and that interpretation must take the form of applying biblical principles to the interpreter's own times and needs.

19 Kendall, p. 74 f.

Breward states this well, highlighting the Christocentric focus of Perkins's hermeneutic. He begins by citing Perkins's contention that Holy Scripture 'agrees with itself most exactly and the places that seem to disagree may easily be reconciled,' for the simple reason that 'the scope of the whole Bible is Christ with his benefits.' If diverse opinions about the meaning of scripture existed:

> In this diversity of opinions ... we must still [always] have recourse to Christ, and that in the scripture alone: for although there were a thousand diverse expositions of one place, yet by the circumstances thereof, conferring [comparing] it with other like places of scripture, a man shall be able to find out the true sense: for Christ *in Scripture expoundeth himself*.[20]

Of the supralapsarian version of Calvinism that Perkins learned from Beza and Zanchius, set forth in *A Golden Chain*, and defended in Latin in *De Praedestinatione* (1598) and in English in *God's Free Grace and Man's Free-will* (1602), little need be said here. Supralapsarianism is the view that in God's initial, pre-mundane decision-making with regard to mankind His purpose of electing some and reprobating the others envisaged human beings not yet created, as distinct from the infralapsarian view that in decreeing this double predestination God envisaged human beings as both created and fallen. Perkins embraced supralapsarianism out of a desire to maintain the absolute sovereignty of God in our salvation against the Lutherans, semipelagian Roman Catholics like Bellarmine, and anti-predestinarians in England like Peter Baro, Samuel Harsnet and William Barrett. By embracing it, however, he surrounded the good news of the redeeming love of God to lost sinners with a forbidding rationalistic framework which, like all versions of

---

20 Breward, p. 47, drawing on Perkins, *Workes*, II.55 f., I.484, III.220; my italics. Breward's review of Perkins's interpretative procedures, as set forth in his pioneer homiletical handbook, *The Art of Prophesying* (1607; in Latin *Prophetica*, 1592), and illustrated by his printed expositions, should by all means be consulted.

the supralapsarian formula, seemed to imply that God is an arbitrary decision-maker with an abstract interest in having two sorts of people, one justly saved and one justly condemned, and that He willed the fall in Eden as a means to this end.[21] Most seventeenth-century Puritans, like most Reformed theologians since their time, were infralapsarian, and it is in order, I think, to express quiet regret that Perkins the Elizabethan Puritan pioneer took a different line. The sovereignty of God in salvation must surely be maintained, but dogmatic supralapsarianism is not the best nor the most scriptural way to do it.

But the supralapsarianism in Perkins's head did not in any way inhibit the expressing of his evangelistic and pastoral heart, and it is to this that I return as I close. From an exposition of Zephaniah 2:1-2, 'preached at Stourbridge Fair, in the field; taken from his mouth'[22] – that is, recorded, presumably in shorthand, as he spoke, apparently in 1593, and published posthumously in 1605 – I draw two extracts, both characteristically Puritan (by which I mean that any Puritan preacher over the next hundred years might have said the same; indeed, we know that very many did). The first extract shows us Perkins the evangelist, proclaiming the whosoever-will invitation of the gospel. Speaking of the gospel promise as a 'precious jewel', Perkins says:

> ... never allege that it is above thy compass and being a jewel is too dear and costly for thee, for I offer it freely unto you and to every one of you. I pronounce unto you from the Lord that here this blessed doctrine is offered unto you all in his name freely and that you may buy it without money (Isa. 55:1). Happy is that day when thou, coming so far to buy things for thy body and paying so dear for them, dost meet with so precious a jewel, the virtue whereof will save thy soul, and payest nothing for it.

---

21 The sharpest statement of this defect is that of B.B. Warfield, *The Plan of Salvation*, (revised ed., Grand Rapids: Eerdmans, 1966), p. 88: 'That (God) has any creatures at all they (the supralapsarians) suppose to be in the interest of discrimination, and all that he decrees concerning his creatures they suppose that he decrees only that he may discriminate between them.'

22 Breward, p. 279.

The second extract is pastoral, prophetic, and in the best sense patriotic. It has to do with England, England's Church, and the threat of national judgment.

> The common sins of England ... are ... First, ignorance of God's will and worship ... The second main sin of England is contempt of Christian religion ...
>
> Our church doubtless is God's cornfield and we are the corn heap of God and those Brownists [followers of Robert Browne who wanted separation] are blinded and besotted who cannot see that the Church of England is a goodly heap of God's corn. But withal we must confess that we are full of chaff ... therefore God will winnow us to find out the corn ... the way to escape God's trial is to try thyself ... and so the way to escape the fearful fan of God is to fan thine own heart by the law of God ... Once a day put thyself and thy life under the fan of God's law ... Once a day keep a court in thy conscience, call thy thoughts, thy words, thy deeds to their trial. Let the ten commandments pass upon them, and thy sins and corruptions which thou findest to be chaff, blow them away by repentance ... Our long peace, plenty and ease have bred great sins ... When we have renewed our repentance, let us then every one of us deal with the Lord by earnest prayer for this church and nation, that the Lord would show his mercy upon it and continue unto it this peace and the gospel.

In the original title of this study I rated William Perkins, theologian, preacher and pastor four centuries ago, an Anglican to remember; and I trust that what we have learned has justified that estimate. I now ask: is there not an uncanny relevance for us in the thoughts about England and the Church of England that we have just found Perkins expressing? And, so we might add, the churches of Scotland, Ireland and Wales. That is a question that I hope we shall all ponder.

Richard Baxter (1615-1691)

A Man for All Ministries

The seventy-six years of Richard Baxter's life spanned an era in English history that was tragic, heroic, and pathetic by turns to an extraordinary degree. It was a time of revolution and counter-revolution in church and state; of brutal religious persecution, of fierce controversy in print about almost everything; of disruptive socio-economic shifts which nobody at the time understood; of widespread bad health, growing towns innocent of hygiene, and nightmarishly primitive medicine; in short, it was a time of hardship for just about everyone. And at the head of the list of factors that led to the tragedies, the heroisms, and the miseries, stood rival understandings of Christianity. That is a sad thing to have to say, but it is true.

Had you been a Christian of consistent principles, whatever they were, living through those seventy-six years, you too would have had a rough ride. If you had been a Roman Catholic, you would have been an object of general distaste in the community all the time, constantly suspected of being a political subversive. Had you been a High Anglican, wedded to the Prayer Book, the ministry of bishops, and the royal supremacy in church and state, you would have watched your side lose the Civil War in the 1640s, you would have wept over the (to you) traitorous act of executing the king for treason against his people, you would have seen Prayer Book and episcopacy at one stage outlawed by Parliament, and if you had been a clergyman you would have lost your living for the best part of twenty years before the Restoration (1660). And if, like Baxter, you had been a Puritan, practising and propagating the religion of St Augustine on the basis of the theology of John Calvin, you would have had to endure the Arminianizing of Anglican leadership for two decades before the Civil War, the ejecting of almost 2,000 Puritan-type clergy from English parishes at the Restoration, the consequent Anglican slide away from the gospel, and the great persecution of Protestant nonconformists that put tens of thousands in gaol for not using the Prayer Book in their worship of God during the quarter century before toleration came in 1689. Whatever your principles, you would have experienced much unhappiness during those years.

A moment ago I called Richard Baxter a Puritan; and since that word still carries prejudicial overtones for many, as it did throughout Baxter's own life, I had better say at once that my reason for using it is simply that it was as a Puritan that Baxter saw himself. Noting in 1680 that two of his opponents in print had called him (in Latin) a dyed-in-the-wool Puritan and one who oozed the whole of Puritanism from every pore, he responded by commenting: 'Alas I am not so good and happy.' Though he was, as we would say, ecumenically oriented, sympathetically alert to all the main Christian traditions and happy to learn from them all, he constantly equated the Puritan ideal with Christianity – 'mere Christianity' to use his own phrase, which C.S. Lewis later borrowed from him – and all his writings display him as the classic mainstream Puritan that he ever sought to be.

What, then, was Puritanism? Matthew Sylvester, the not-too-competent editor of Baxter's posthumous narrative of his life and times (published as *Reliquiae Baxterianae*, 800 folio pages, 1696) notes in his preface that in matters of history, as in everything else, Baxter had: 'an Eagle's Eye, an Honest Heart, a thoughtful Soul, a searching and considerate (i.e., reflective) Spirit, and a concerned frame of Mind to let the present and succeeding Generations duly know the real and true state and issues' of things:[1] what description of Puritanism, then, would Baxter have acknowledged as fair and true? The question is not too hard to answer. Puritanism, as Baxter understood it and as modern scholarship, correcting centuries of caricature, now depicts it, was a total view of Christianity, Bible-based, church-centred, God-honouring, literate, orthodox, pastoral, and Reformational, that saw personal, domestic, professional, political, churchly, and economic existence as aspects of a single whole, and that called on everybody to order every department and every relationship of their life according to the Word of God, so that all would be sanctified and become 'holiness to the Lord'. Puritanism's spearhead activity was pastoral evangelism and nurture through preaching, catechizing, and counselling (which the Puritans themselves called casuistry), and Puritan teaching harped constantly on the themes of self-knowledge, self-humbling, and repentance; faith in, and love for, Jesus Christ the Saviour; the necessity of regeneration, and of sanctification (holy living, by God's power) as proof of it; the need of conscientious conformity to all God's law, and for a disciplined use of the means of grace; and the blessedness of the assurance and joy from the Holy Spirit that all faithful believers under ordinary circumstances may know. Puritans saw themselves as God's pilgrims, travelling home, God's warriors, battling against the world, the flesh, and the devil, and God's servants, under orders to share Christ, impart godliness, and comprehensively do all the good they could as they went along. This was the Christianity with which Baxter identified, and of which he was a shining example throughout the vicissitudes of his own long life.

1 Preface to *Reliquiae Baxterianae* (*RB*), 1696, sec. 2, p. 2.

II

Let us get a little closer to Baxter. Here are the key personal facts, summarised in *Who's Who* fashion. With a few intrusions as we move through them, they are as follows:

'Baxter, Richard, gentleman' (for his father owned a small estate); 'born 12 November 1615, at Rowton, Salop; educated at Donnington Free School, Wroxeter, and privately' (Baxter never went to a university); 'ordained deacon by Bishop of Worcester, 1638; curate of Bridgnorth, 1639-40; lecturer' – that is, salaried preacher – 'of Kidderminster, 1641-42; with the Parliamentary army, 1642-47; vicar of Kidderminster, 1647-61' – a ministry during which he just about converted the whole town – 'at Savoy Conference, 1661' (this was the abortive consultation between Puritan and Anglican leaders for the improving of the Prayer Book for the restored Church of England); 'lived privately in or near London, 1662-91; married Margaret Charlton (1636-81), 1662; imprisoned for one week in Clerkenwell gaol, 1669, for twenty-one months in Southwark gaol, 1685-86; died 8 December, 1691; author of *The Saints' Everlasting Rest* (1650)' – an all-time devotional classic on how thoughts of God and heaven can renew the heart for service here below, an 800 page volume that sold an edition a year for the first decade of its life; *The Reformed Pastor* (1656) – another all-time classic, admonishing, motivating, and instructing the clergy; *A Call to the Unconverted* (1658)– the first evangelistic pocket-book in English, which in its year of publication sold 20,000 copies, and brought an unending stream of readers to faith during Baxter's lifetime; *A Christian Directory* (1673) – a unique million-plus-word compendium of Puritan teaching about Christian life and conduct; 'and over 130 other books; special interests, pastoral care, Christian unity; hobbies, medicine, science, history.' Such was the man we are now commemorating.

Is it important for later generations to remember Baxter? In 1875 in Kidderminster they thought it was, and a fine statue of him preaching was erected in the town centre, with the following inscription:

BETWEEN THE YEARS 1641 AND 1660
THIS TOWN WAS THE SCENE OF THE LABOURS
OF
RICHARD BAXTER
RENOWNED EQUALLY FOR HIS CHRISTIAN
LEARNING
AND PASTORAL FIDELITY.
IN A STORMY AND DIVIDED AGE
HE ADVOCATED UNITY AND COMPREHENSION
POINTING THE WAY TO THE EVERLASTING
REST.
CHURCHMEN AND NONCONFORMISTS
UNITED TO RAISE THE MEMORIAL, A.D. 1875.

The phrases used show what it was about Baxter that was thought worth remembering in 1875. 'Christian learning', for instance, points to the fact that he was in fact an omnivorous polymath, always studying, reading quickly, and remembering well what he had read, and consistently thoughtful and discerning in the opinions he expressed on what the books set before him. Once he complained that the loss of time for study due to his many illnesses (for he was a sick man all his life) was the greatest burden he had to bear; anyone, however, who observes his mastery of biblical material, of the entire Christian tradition, and of the dozens of positions that he controverts, will marvel at the amount of studying that he actually accomplished. He was in fact the most voluminous English theologian of all time, and in addition to the approximately four million words of pastoral, apologetic, devotional and homiletic writing that are reprinted in his *Practical Works* he produced about six million more on aspects of the doctrine of grace and salvation, church unity and nonconformity, the sacraments, Roman Catholicism, antinomianism, millenarianism, Quakerism, politics and history, not to mention a systematic theology in Latin; and in all of these writings, whether or not one finally agrees with Baxter's positions, one finds oneself confronted with the mature judgment of a clear, sharp, well-stocked, wise mind, as distinguished for intellectual integrity as for spiritual alertness. I do not think Baxter was always right, but I see him, as did the memorials of 1875, as one of the most impressive of Christian thinkers, and I urge that there is just as much reason to honour him as such today as there was those many years ago.

Then, again, the 1875 inscription celebrates Baxter's constant pleas, uttered both *viva voce* and in print over more than forty years, for 'unity and comprehension'. In his own day, Baxter's pleading on these topics went unheeded, partly because of the sharpness of the rhetoric in which much of it was couched, but mainly because it was an age in which party spirit and dog-eat-dog wrangling were taken as proper signs of Christian seriousness. By 1875, however, the basic right-mindedness of what Baxter was saying had become apparent, and it ought to be even more apparent today. Baxter's call to unity depended on distinguishing tolerable from intolerable differences among professing Christians and churches; his plea was, first, that all love, peace and communion should be maximised on the basis that in reality all Christian essentials are already held by those who accept the Apostles' Creed, the Ten Commandments and the Lord's Prayer, as fixing the shape of their Christianity, and, second, that all would henceforth observe the maxim, unity in necessary things, liberty in non-necessary things and charity in all things. Baxter's call for comprehension depended on his view of the Church of England as being what its first Reformers saw it as – namely, a federation of congregations standing for 'mere Christianity', that is, a Christianity defined in terms of the essentials and no more, and committed together to the task of evangelising and discipling the English. Here, his plea was for a relaxation of the restored Anglican uniformity of 1662 that would allow Presbyterian, Independent, and Baptist groups a place within the federation, for the furtherance of the common calling. His reasoning was noble and cogent in itself, and more than timely during those years in which all nonconformists (120,000 or so, according to one estimate) faced fines and imprisonment if they were caught worshipping in company in their own way. Baxter's pitch was queered by Anglican hatred and suspicion of nonconformists as being all revolutionaries at heart, by the prevalence among Anglicans of High Church theology which saw non-episcopal churches as no churches and their ministers as no ministers, and by nonconformist bitterness and contempt of the persecuting Church of England, and unwillingness ever to associate with it again, so that in the event his argumentation was ignored by all parties throughout his lifetime. But we can see why in 1875, before the hurricanes of unbelief laid waste great sections of both the Free Church and the Anglican worlds and permanently changed the shape of the comprehension issue, the memorialists wished to celebrate the witness Baxter had borne.

And what, now, of ourselves? Are Baxter's theological attainments, and pastoral strengths, and arguments for unity and comprehension, and testimonies to the supreme importance of fixing one's hopes on the saints' everlasting rest, worth our remembrance today? I maintain not only are they worth remembering in themselves as inspiring examples of vision, vitality and wisdom in Christ, but that Baxter has more to say, and to give, to those who remember him in our day, than was the case with the men and women of 1875, just because we have drifted further from that vision, vitality, and wisdom than they had. The title of this chapter is 'A Man for All Ministries'. I propose to spend the rest of my time looking more closely at Baxter the man and at the serving roles that he fulfilled, and my suggestion at each point will be that we today need to learn from him in the way that small, superficial, shallow people always need to learn from the giants. To this agenda I now turn.

III

Often described as seraphic, because of the way that his rhetoric soars when he is dilating on the grace of God and the blessings of the gospel, Baxter appears throughout his ministry as the very epitome of single-minded ardour in seeking the glory of God through the salvation of souls and the sanctification of the church. To contemplate the independence, integrity, and zeal with which the public Baxter fulfilled his ministry is fascinating and inspiring; but even more fascinating and inspiring, to my mind at any rate, is contemplation of the private Baxter, the man behind the ministry, who in an elaborate self-analysis, written it seems about 1665, when he was fifty, and published posthumously as part of his *Reliquiae*, opens his heart about the changes he sees in himself since his younger years in Christian service. In general, what he delineates is a progress from raw zeal to ripe simplicity, and from a passionate narrowness that was somewhat self-absorbed and majored in minors to a calm concentration on God and the big things, and a profound capacity to see those big things steadily and whole. I subjoin some extracts from this gem of humble, honest witness to the transforming work of God in a human life so that you may get the flavour of Baxter directly, and judge for yourself whether I exaggerate in which I have just said.[2]

> I have perceived that nothing so much hindereth the reception of the truth as urging it on men with too harsh importunity, and falling too heavily on their errors.
>
> In my youth I was quickly past my fundamentals and was running up into a multitude of controversies ... But the elder I grew the smaller the stress I laid upon those controversies and curiosities (though still my intellect abhorreth confusion) . . .. And now it is the fundamental doctrines of the Catechism which I highliest value and daily think of, and find most useful to myself and others. The Creed, the Lord's Prayer and the Ten Commandments do find me now the most acceptable and plentiful matter for all my meditations. They are to me as my daily bread and drink ... I value all things according to their use and ends, and I find in the daily practice and experience of my soul that the knowledge of God and Christ, and the Holy Spirit,

2 Quotations are from *The Autobiography of Richard Baxter*, ed. J. M. Lloyd Thomas, (London: J. M. Dent, 1931), pp. 106, 107 f, 112, 115, 117, 118 f, 125, 130 f. This abridgment of *RB* was re-edited by N. H. Keeble, (London: J.M. Dent, Everyman's Library, 1974).

and the truth of Scripture, and the life to come, and of a holy life, is of more use to me than all the most curious speculations ... That is the best doctrine and study which maketh men better and tendeth to make them happy ...

Heretofore I placed much of religion in tenderness of heart, and grieving for sin, and penitential tears ... but my conscience now looketh at love and delight in God, and praising him, as the top of all my religious duties ...

My judgement is much more for frequent and serious meditation on the heavenly blessedness than it was heretofore in my younger days ... now I had rather read, hear or meditate on God and heaven than on any other subject ... I was once wont to meditate on my own heart ... poring either on my sins or wants, or examining my sincerity; but now, though I am greatly convinced of the need of heart-aquaintance ... I see more need of a higher work, and that I should look often upon Christ and God and heaven, (rather) than upon my own heart.

I now see more good and more evil in all men than heretofore I did ... I less admire gifts of utterance and bare profession of religion than I once did ... I once thought that almost all that could pray movingly and fluently, and talk well of religion, had been saints. But experience hath opened to me what odious crimes may consist with high profession ...

I was wont to look but little further than England in my prayers, as not considering the rest of the world ... But now, as I better understand the case of the world and the method of the Lord's Prayer ... no part of my prayers are so deeply serious as that for the conversion of the infidel and ungodly world ...

(He goes on to express admiration for the missionary pioneer John Eliot, 'the apostle of the Indians in New England', whose work he helped to support financially, and to voice the wish that all 2,000 Puritan clergy ejected in 1662 could have become overseas missionaries.)

I am deeplier afflicted for the disagreements of Christians than I was when I was a younger Christian. Except the case of the

> infidel world, nothing is so sad and grievous to my thoughts as the case of the divided churches. And therefore I am more deeply sensible of the sinfulness of those prelates and pastors of the churches who are the principal cause of these divisions. The contentions between the Greek Church and the Roman, the Papists and the Protestants, the Lutherans and the Calvinists, have woefully hindered the kingdom of Christ.
>
> Though my works were never such as could be any temptation to me to dream of obliging God by proper merit in commutative justice, yet one of the most ready, constant, undoubted evidences of my ... interest in his covenant is the consciousness of my living as devoted to him. And I the easilier believe the pardon of my failings through my Redeemer while I know that I serve no other master, and that I know no other end, or trade, or business, but that I am imployed [*sic*] in his work, and make it the business of my life, and live to him in the world, notwithstanding my infirmities. And this bent and business of my life, with my longing desires after perfection in the knowledge and belief and love of God, and in a holy and heavenly mind and life, are the two standing, constant, discernible evidences which most put me out of doubt of my sincerity. (He means, of his being truly regenerate and born again.)
>
> And though I before told of the change of my judgement against provoking writings, I have had more will than skill since to avoid such. I must mention it by way of penitent confession, that I am too much inclined to such words in controversial writings which are too keen, and apt to provoke the person whom I write against ... And therefore I repent of it, and wish all over-sharp passages were expunged from my writings, and desire forgiveness of God and man.

It is surely apparent that these are the words of a great and holy man, naturally gifted and supernaturally sanctified beyond most, humble, patient, realistic and frank to a very unusual degree. The quiet peace and joy that shine through these almost clinical observations on himself are truly impressive; here is an endlessly active man whose soul is at rest in God all the time as he labours in prayer Godward and in persuasion manward. And the poise of his spirit is the more impressive when we recall that of all the great Puritan sufferers – and the Puritans as a body were great sufferers – none had a heavier load of pain and provocation to endure than did he. He suffered throughout his adult life from a multitude of bodily ailments (a tubercular cough; frequent nosebleeds and bleeding from his finger-ends; migraine headaches; inflamed eyes; all kinds of digestive disorders; kidney stones and gallstones; and more), so that from the age of twenty-one he was, as he says, 'seldom an hour free from pain', and expected death constantly through the next fifty-five years of partial disablement before his release finally came. Then, after 1662, he suffered a great deal of hatred and harassment because he was a prominent nonconformist leader: this led to several arrests for preaching, some spells in prison, the distraining (confiscation) of his goods to pay fines, including on one occasion the very bed on which he was lying sick, and finally a trial, if it can be called that, before the appalling Judge Jeffreys, Lord Chief Justice of England (answerable therefore to no one) and James II's human whip for flaying rebels. This was the lowest point of public degradation that Baxter was ever reduced to, and it is worth pausing to get a glimpse of it.[3]

The charge was sedition: a ridiculous, trumped-up accusation based on expository words in his *Paraphrase of the New Testament* about the Pharisees and Jewish authorities, into which was read an attack on England's rulers in church and state. (Baxter later commented that by the same logic he could have been indicted for uttering the words, 'Deliver us from evil,' in the Lord's Prayer.) Jeffreys would not let Baxter and his six legal representatives say anything coherent at any stage, and the disputed passages in the *Paraphrase* were never discussed; Jeffreys simply ranted on against the seventy-year-old Puritan veteran as (these are the words of an eye-witness) 'a conceited, stubborn, fanatical dog, that did not conform when he might have been preferred (that is, been

3 The details are from an eye-witness account reproduced in *Autobiography*, pp. 258-64.

a bishop: Baxter was offered the see of Hereford at the Restoration) hang him! This one old fellow hath cast more reproach upon the constitution and excellent discipline of our Church than will be wiped out this hundred years ... by God! He deserves to be whipped through the city.' When the judge had finished haranguing the jury, Baxter said: 'Does your lordship think any jury will pretend to pass a verdict on me upon such a trial?' 'I'll warrant you, Mr Baxter,' replied Jeffreys; 'don't you trouble yourself about that.' And the jury promptly found him guilty without retiring. The result for Baxter was eighteen months in gaol.

It should be added, however, that after Baxter was dead at seventy-six, and Jeffreys had drunk himself into the grave at the age of forty, and it was known that Matthew Sylvester was to be Baxter's biographer, Tillotson, the Archbishop of Canterbury, wrote Sylvester a letter of encouragement containing the following sentences about the trial:

> 'Nothing more honourable than when the Rev. Baxter stood at bay, berogued (slandered), abused, despised; and never more great than then. Draw this well ... This is the noblest part of his life, and not that he might have been a bishop. The Apostle (2 Cor. 11) when he would glory, mentions his labours and strifes and bonds and imprisonments: his troubles, weariness, dangers, reproaches; not his riches and coaches and advantages. God lead us into this spirit and free us from the worldly one which we are apt to run into.'[4]

One can only say: Amen to that.

IV

We have seen something of Baxter the man; let us now look at some of the ministering roles he fulfilled. First, I focus on Baxter as an evangelistic and pastoral communicator – preacher, teacher, and writer.

The best curtain-raiser for this section is Baxter's own account of the fruitfulness of his Kidderminster ministry. He found the

4 Quoted from *Autobiography*, p. 298.

town's 2,000 adults 'an ignorant, rude, and revelling people, for the most part ... they had hardly ever had any lively serious preaching among them.' Soon, however, things began to happen.

> When I first entered upon my Labours in the Ministry I took special notice of everyone that was humbled, reformed or converted; but when I had laboured long, it pleased God that the Converts were so many, that I could not afford time for such particular Observations ... Families and considerable Numbers at once ... came in and grew up I scarce knew how ...
>
> The Congregation was usually full, so that we were fain to build five Galleries after my coming hither ... The Church would have held about a thousand without the galleries. Our private Meetings (small groups, as we would nowadays call them) were also full. On the Lord's Day (which had been sports day before Baxter arrived) there was no disorder to be seen in the streets, but you might hear an hundred Families singing Psalms and repeating Sermons, as you passed through the Streets. In a word, when I came thither first, there was about one Family in a Street that worshipped God and called on His Name, and when I came away there were some streets where there was not past one Family in the side of a Street that did not so; and that did not by professing serious Godliness, give us hopes of their sincerity ... When I set upon Personal Conference and Catechising them, there were very few families in all the Town that refused to come ... (Baxter asked them to call on him at home, since his bad health constantly disabled him from visiting their homes). And few families went from me without some tears, or seemingly serious promises of a Godly Life.[5]

What was the secret of Baxter's success (so far, at least, as this can be analysed in terms of means to ends)? He notes, as significant factors in the situation, that his people had not been gospel-hardened; that he had good helpers, both assistant clergy and members of the flock; that his converts' holy living was winsome while the town's black sheep made sin appear most repulsive;

5 *RB*, part 1, pp. 21, 84 f.

that Kidderminster was free of rival congregations and sectarian bickerings; that most of the families were at home most of the time, working as weavers, so that they had 'time enough to read or talk of holy Things ... as they stand in their Loom they can set a Book before them or edify one another.'[6] Also, it was helpful (Baxter continues) that he fulfilled a long ministry; that he practised church discipline; that, being unmarried, he could concentrate on serving his people; that he gave out Bibles and books (he received every fifteenth copy of each of his own books in lieu of royalties for free distribution); that he gave money to the needy; and that he fulfilled for a time the role of amateur physician – effectively, it seems, and without charge – until he could persuade a qualified doctor to move to the town. He held that all these factors helped the gospel forward, and no doubt he was right. But the key element in his success, humanly speaking, was undoubtedly the clarity, force, and skill with which he communicated the gospel itself.

The content of Baxter's gospel was not in any way distinctive. It was the historic Puritan, evangelical, New Testament message of ruin, redemption, and regeneration. Baxter called for conversion from the life of thoughtless self-centredness and sin to Jesus Christ, the crucified Saviour and risen Lord, and he spelt out in great detail what this must mean in terms of repentance, faith, and new obedience. He saw the unconverted as on the road to hell, and as spiritually asleep in the sense of not recognising their danger, so he set himself both in the pulpit and in his annual personal conversation ('catechising', as he called it) with each family of the parish, to wake them up and persuade them to thoroughgoing Christian commitment before it was too late. What he said, and how he said it, may be learned from his classic writings on conversion, among them *A Treatise of Conversion*, *Directions and Persuasions to a Sound Conversion*, and *A Call to the Unconverted* (full title: *A Call to the Unconverted to Turn and Live, and Accept of Mercy while Mercy may be Had, as ever they*

6 *RB*, part 1, p. 89.

would find Mercy in the Day of their Extremity: from the Living God): all of these were originally sermons preached in series to Baxter's Kidderminster congregation.

Baxter observes that personal conversion had not been dealt with by any of his predecessors in the detail in which he himself set it forth. He displays it very fully as a process whereby, under the light of constant instruction about faith, repentance and true life in Christ, new creation – regeneration, that is, according to this word's later usage – takes place secretly in the human heart, and shows itself by first desiring and then seeking Jesus Christ, and continuing to reach out towards Him and open one's life to Him and invoke His promises and adore His mercy till one knows that one has found Him (or, putting it more accurately, knows that one has been found by Him). After this the converted person will continue to walk with Christ in discipleship, learning and obeying, loving and serving, worshipping Him and working for Him in peace and joy. Though realisation of the Saviour's nearness, and consequent change in thought and behaviour, may be sudden, as it was for Paul on the Damascus road and has been for many since, the process as a whole takes time, and it is God, not the evangelist, who decides how quickly or slowly it will advance, and when it will come to fruition. Baxter holds it all together – the sovereign grace of God, the renewal of the heart, the need to teach and learn the faith with maximum seriousness and urgency because of the eternal issues at stake, and the importance of constant evangelistic endeavour in every Christian congregation. Much of the minister's proper practice as a pastoral evangelist, as Baxter saw it, is spelled out in his classic exposition, *The Reformed Pastor*, in which his practical conversion-centredness exhibits itself to the full.

Nor was this all. In 1664, no longer permitted to pastor a congregation, his mind went back to urgings by the late Archbishop Usher that he should 'write a directory for the several ranks of professed Christians' and to a long-standing plan of his own to write 'a family directory.' In the course of a year he produced a treatise of a million and a quarter words, which when published in 1673 bore the title:

A CHRISTIAN DIRECTORY
Or
A Sum of Practical Theology, and Cases of Conscience
Directing Christians
How to Use their Knowledge and Faith;
How to Improve all Helps and Means, and how to Perform all Duties;
How to Overcome Temptations, and to Escape or Mortify Every Sin;
In Four Parts.
I Christian Ethics (or Private Duties)
II Christian Economics (or Family Duties)
III Christian Ecclesiastics (or Church Duties)
IV Christian Politics (or Duties to our Rulers and Neighbours)

Baxter's first chapter, however, is headed: 'Directions to Unconverted, Graceless Sinners, for the Attainment of Saving Grace,' and the second is: 'Directions to Weak Christians for their Establishment and Growth.' Thus the essential perspective of this compendium stands revealed: *A Christian Directory* is, precisely, a mammoth treatise on the converted life.

We should not suppose that conversion was Baxter's only theme in his Kidderminster ministry. He himself tells us that he ranged much wider:

> 'The thing which I daily opened to them, and with the greatest importunity laboured to imprint upon their minds, was the great Fundamental Principles of Christianity contained in their Baptismal Covenant, even a right knowledge, and belief of, and subjection and love to, God the Father, the Son, and the Holy Ghost; and Love to all Men, and Concord with the Church and one another: I did so daily inculcate the Knowledge of God our Creator, Redeemer, and Sanctifier, and Love and Obedience to God, and Unity with the Church Catholick, and Love to Men,

> and Hope of Life Eternal, that these were the matter of their daily Cogitations and Discourses, and indeed their Religion.'[7]

But Baxter was an evangelist, and he constantly led his hears back to the life-and-death question: will you, or will you not, turn and live? Will you now take seriously the things you say you believe about sin, and Christ, and heaven, and hell?

Here is a sample of Baxter's evangelistic rhetoric as he applies a message on Hebrews 11:1:, 'Faith is the substance of things hoped for, the evidence of things not seen.' He has made the point that faith treats as real the realities of which Scripture speaks: God, Christ, Satan; the final judgment, heaven, and hell. He has pressed the question: 'Are you in good earnest, when you say, you believe in a heaven and hell? And do you think, and speak, and pray, and live, as those that do indeed believe it? ... Deal truly ... if you would know where you must live for ever, know how, and for what, and upon what it is that you live here.' He has invited his hearers to think what difference it would make to them if they could actually see, with their physical eyes, Christ, their own forthcoming death, judgment day, with Satan accusing, and the condition of those already experiencing heaven and hell. Now he pins the congregation to the wall.[8]

> ... Answer these following questions, upon the foregoing suppositions.
>
> 1. If you saw but what you say you do believe, would you not be convinced that the most pleasant, gainful sin is worse than madness? And would you not spit at the very name of it?
>
> 2. What would you think of the most serious, holy life, if you had seen the things you say you do believe? Would you ever again reproach it as preciseness [a long-standing contemptuous label for the Puritan lifestyle] or count it more ado than needs, and think your time were better spent in playing than

7 *RB*, part 1, p. 93 f.

8 *Practical Works* (Ligonier PA: Soli Deo Gloria, 1991), III. p. 585 f.

> in praying; in drinking, and sports, and filthy lusts, than in the holy services of the Lord? ...
>
> 3. If you saw but what you say you do believe, would you ever again be offended with the ministers of Christ for the plainest reproofs, and closest exhortations, and strictest precepts and discipline ...? Then you would understand what moved ministers to be so importunate with you for conversion; and whether trifling or serious preaching was the best.
>
> 4. ... I durst then ask the worst that heareth me, Dare you now be drunk, or gluttonous, or worldly? Dare you be voluptuous, proud, or fornicators any more? Dare you go home, and make a jest at piety, and neglect your souls, as you have done? ...
>
> 8. And oh how such a sight would advance the Redeemer, and his grace, and promises, and word, and ordinances in your esteem! It would quicken your desires, and make you fly to Christ for life, as a drowning man to that which may support him. How sweetly then would you relish the name, the word, the ways of Christ, which now seem dry and common things!'

That is vintage Baxter, arousing the complacent. It remains only to add that he was preaching before King Charles II, England's merry monarch, and his merry court, and that the sermon was in fact published by royal command, though not, it seems, heeded by royal conscience. The quality that the 1875 inscription calls 'pastoral fidelity' made Baxter willing to say 'boo' to any goose, even a royal one. That was the kind of preacher he was.

The second sphere of Baxter's ministry at which we glance is the field of ecclesiastical statesmanship, where Baxter, the advocate of a comprehensive national church, as we saw, was in constant action after 1662 negotiating for agreement with the Independents and a rapprochement with the Church of England, and writing documents and publishing books to that end. Not much need be said about this, because it was an area in which he did not shine at all and finally achieved nothing. His provocative manner in discussion and debate totally thwarted his unitive purpose. His schoolmasterly strictures upon the cherished beliefs of others only made enemies. As the sermon just quoted would suggest, he was too blunt and oracular in style to be a bridge-builder. The position from which he reached out in all these discussions, however, was a non-sectarian, noble one, which when applying for a licence to preach under the royal Indulgence of 1672 he formulated as follows:[9]

> My religion is merely Christian; but as rejecting the Papal Monarchy and its attendant evils, I am a Protestant.
>
> The rule of my faith and doctrine is the law of God in Nature and Scripture.
>
> The Church which I am a member of is the Universality of Christians, in conjunction with all particular churches of Christians in England or elsewhere in the world, whose communion according to my capacity I desire.

Sometimes he called this position, 'Catholicism against all sects'. In his day it was thought eccentric; in ours, it might appear as prophetic, marking the path whereby the exclusiveness of denominationalism comes to be transcended. It was never correct to call Baxter a Presbyterian, as was often done; nor after 1662 could one call him an Anglican; he was a 'mere nonconformist' in relation to the Anglican settlement, and that, denominationally speaking, was all. In an ecumenical age it is worth reflecting on the significance of Baxter's non-denominational stance.

A further sphere of ministry in which Baxter moved was the delineating of Christian social justice, and here he shows great skill in reforming medieval formulae and bringing them up to date for seventeenth-century Protestant use. Part IV of the *Christian Directory*, comprising about 200,000 words, deals in detail with rulers and subjects, lawyers, physicians, schoolmasters, soldiers, murder and suicide, scandal, theft, contracts, borrowing, buying and selling, the charging of interest (i.e., usury), wages, landlords and tenants, law-suits, distilling

9 *Autobiography*, p. 293.

out practical guidance for serving and pleasing God in all these relationships, by managing them as expressions of neighbour-love and cooperative service, and avoiding any form of callous or careless exploitation. One must not try, he says, 'to get another's goods or labour for less than it is worth,' nor must one make profit out of the customer's ignorance or necessity: 'it is a false rule of them that think a commodity is worth so much as anyone will give' for it. 'To wish to buy cheap and sell dear is common (as St Augustine observes), but it is a common vice.'[10] And landlords must not squeeze rents so that tenants cannot live decently, or have leisure to care for their souls. This point Baxter made again, later, in a separate tract, *The Poor Husbandman's Advocate to Rich Racking Landlords*, which he finished only six weeks before his death (it was his last writing), and which did not in fact see the light of day till this century.[11]

I wish that space allowed me to explore the idyll of Baxter's marriage, a 19-year partnership with a brilliant woman, twenty-one years younger than himself, whom he memorialised in an account of her life written 'under the power of melting Grief' a few weeks after her death in 1681. The account was well and lovingly edited by J. T. Wilkinson in 1928 under the title *Richard Baxter and Margaret Charlton: A Puritan Love-Story,* and I myself edited a version of it, with essays on Puritan marriage and the managing of grief, under the title *A Grief Sanctified*, in 2002. 'When we were married,' writes Baxter, 'her sadness and melancholy vanished: counsel did something to it, and contentment something; and being taken up with our household affairs did somewhat. And we lived in inviolated love and mutual complacency sensible of the benefit of mutual help.' Baxter's account of his wife's ministry to him has in it many such hints of his ministry as a husband to her, and it is evident that in this

10 *Puritanism and Richard Baxter,* Hugh Martin, (London: SCM Press, 1954), p. 173.

11 Published as *The Reverend Richard Baxter's Last Treatise*, ed. F. J. Powicke (Manchester: John Rylands Library, 1926).

he did well, although he writes of himself, with that devastating perfectionist honesty that we saw in him before: 'My dear wife did look for more good in me than she found, especially lately in my weakness and decay. We are all like pictures that must not be looked on too near. They that come near us find more faults and badness in us than others at a distance know.'[12] Well, maybe so; yet if one picks up all the hints in the narrative, Baxter's marital ministry appears as something to be very much admired, and in days like ours to be viewed as something of a model. His wife, though a passionately devoted Christian of great enterprise and intelligence, was highly strung and obsessive to a fault, so that living with her would not have been easy. But that theme cannot be pursued here.

V

It was usual to end Puritan funeral sermons with a reference to the dead person's final hours; for it was an age in which people died at home, in company, without pain-killing drugs, and often in full consciousness to the very end, and it was taken for granted that their dying behaviour and their last words, spoken from the edge of eternity, would have special significance for those whom they left behind. This is not a funeral sermon, but a celebratory essay; nonetheless it is, I think, fitting to end it in this Puritan way. So let it be said that on the day before he died, as on every day of his life, it seems, for the previous forty and more years, Baxter was meditating on heaven, focusing on the description of the heavenly Jerusalem in Hebrews 12:22-24, a passage which, so he told two of his visitors, 'deserves a thousand, thousand thoughts'; and that he told those same visitors, 'I have peace; I have peace'; and that he brushed aside praise for his books with words of almost arrogant humility, 'I was a pen in God's hand; what praise is due to a pen?'; and that his last words, spoken through pain, to Matthew Sylvester, whose

12 *Richard Baxter and Margaret Charlton*, ed. J. T. Wilkinson, (London: George Allen and Unwin, 1928), pp. 110, 152. *A Grief Sanctified*, ed. J. I. Packer, (Wheaton, IL: Crossway, 2002), pp. 90, 127.

pastoral assistant he had been for the previous four years, were: 'Oh I thank him, I thank him. The Lord teach you to die.' And let it further be said that Sylvester himself, preaching Baxter's memorial sermon on Elisha's words, 'Where is the Lord God of Elijah?', was constrained to end by looking ahead to resurrection day (which, of course, for God's people will be reunion day also), and to ask aloud:

> What must I do to meet with our Elijah and his God in peace? Must not my eye be inward, upward, forward, backward, round about? Must I not endeavour to know my errand, warrant, difficulties, duties and encouragements? Must I not ... tell what I believe? ... practice what I preach? And promote the Christian interest with all wisdom, diligence, and faithfulness, as my predecessor did before me?[13]

Baxter's brand of spiritual straightforwardness in the service of the triune God regularly affects Christians as it affected Sylvester; it makes one seek to be energetic and businesslike in one's discipleship and service, just as he was, and gives one a conscience about aimlessness, and casualness, and spiritual drift. For this reason alone it is good for us to remember Baxter, and I have counted it a privilege to be able to introduce you to him in this all-too-sketchy way. From my own acquaintance with him, which now goes back almost seventy years, I say to you all – clergy, layfolk, young Christians, senior Christians – get to know Baxter and stay with Baxter. He will always do you good.

13 Matthew Sylvester, *Elisha's Cry after Elijah's God*, appended to *RB*, p. 18.

EPILOGUE

THE PURITAN PASTOR'S PROGRAMME

I

It is a truth periodically voiced by a few, though rarely heeded by the many, that the church of God on earth, always and everywhere, is just one generation from extinction. Shocking as this may sound, it is not a dictum that is difficult to defend. Should clergy no longer spend their strength teaching the faith, preaching the gospel, and seeking the salvation of souls; should believing parents no longer labour to share their faith with their children, and believers with their neighbours; should the practice of evangelism be abandoned; should the Bible and Christian books be left around the house unread; and should church people settle for being the nicest persons in the world according to the world's specifications; how long do you think the church would remain a going concern? More than a generation? I doubt it. And have you not noticed that much of Western Christianity is currently treading this path to extinction? It seems clearly so to me. What then can stop the rot and turn the tide? One thing only, in my view: a renewed embrace of the Puritan ideal of ministerial service. Without this, nothing can stop the drift downhill.

In saying this, I target specifically what I call the Old West: that is, the primary Protestant groupings from Reformational days, Lutheran, Anglican, Presbyterian and Baptist, in Western Europe, North America, Australasia and South Africa. In central Africa and Asia, it would seem that the Puritan ideal has already been learned from the Scriptures and is being actively implemented in face of much hostility and heavy cultural opposition, particularly from Islam. But now contrast that with our post-Christian, secularised, materialistic, arrogant, drifting Western world. Here the Christian message is mocked, the church is marginalised and ghettoised, and too many clergy persons see their role in explicitly defensive terms, as keeping the institutional wheels going round, if they can, and keeping their congregations feeling good, again if they can. Some find these tasks beyond them; then funding fails, buildings close, congregations disperse, and they themselves move out of pastoral ministry to attempt something else. Others soldier on to retirement, and finish their course thankful for their pensions and otherwise carefree. Meantime, however, the overall situation remains dire, and the sense that as congregations grow older and smaller the church slides further into terminal decline becomes stronger and stronger.

It would seem that the clergy, the church's spiritual leaders, have largely lost their way, and when the leadership loses its way there is small hope for the rank and file. Now what I urge here is that the Puritan ideal for pastors, which, judged by the New Testament Scriptures on which it is based, has classic status in itself, is the foundational reality on which all ventures in church renewal must be based, otherwise they will fail continually until finally all is lost. Let me try to justify this opinion as I close.

II

How should we formulate for ourselves the Puritan pastoral ideal? The foregoing pages have already blocked it in general terms, but for the acme of full-scale, crystallised precision on this, as on so many other matters, we cannot do better than turn to John Owen, by common consent the greatest Puritan theologian and perhaps the greatest British theologian of all time. In a chapter entitled, 'The especial duty of pastors of churches,' in his late treatise, *The True Nature of a Gospel Church* (1689), he sets out the pastor's God-taught job description as follows:

1. The first and principal duty of a pastor is to *feed the flock* by diligent preaching of the Word … . A man is a pastor unto them whom he feeds by pastoral teaching …

   Sundry things are required unto this work and duty of pastoral preaching; as, – (1) Spiritual wisdom and understanding in the mysteries of the gospel … (2) *Experience of the power of the truth* which they preach in and upon their own souls. Without this they will themselves be lifeless and heartless … a man preacheth that sermon only well unto others which preacheth itself in his own soul … If the Word do not dwell with power *in* us, it will not pass with power *from* us. (3) *Skill to divide the Word aright*, 2 Tim. 2:15; and this consists in a practical wisdom, upon a diligent attendance unto the Word of truth, to find out what is real, substantial and meet food for the souls of the hearers, – to give unto all sorts of persons in the church that which is their proper portion. And this requires, (4) *A prudent and diligent consideration* of the state of the flock … as unto their strength or weakness, their growth or defect in knowledge (the measure of their attainments requiring either milk or strong meat), their temptings and duties, their spiritual decays or thrivings; and that not only in general, but, as near as may be, with respect unto all the individual members of the church … And, (5) All these … are to be constantly accompanied with the evidence of *zeal for the glory of God* and *compassion for the souls of men*. Where these are not in vigorous exercise in the minds and souls of them that preach the Word, giving a demonstration of themselves unto the consciences of them that hear, the quickening form, the life and soul of preaching, is lost.

2. The second duty of a pastor towards his flock is continual fervent prayer for them, James 5:16; John 17:20; Exodus 32:11;

Deuteronomy 9:18; Leviticus 16:24; 1 Samuel 12:23; 2 Corinthians 13:7, 9; Ephesians 1:15-19, 3:14; Philippians 1:4; Colossians 1:3; 2 Thessalonians 1:11 ... In this constant prayer for the church, which is so incumbent on all pastors as that whatever is done without it is of no esteem in the sight of Jesus Christ, respect is to be had, (1) Unto *the success of the Word*, unto all the blessed ends of it, among them. These are no less than the improvement and strengthening of all their graces, the direction of all their duties, their edification in faith and love, with the entire conduct of their souls in the life of God, unto the enjoyment of him ... (2) Unto *the temptations that the church is generally exposed unto* ... (3) Unto *the especial state and condition of all the members* ... (4) Unto *the presence of Christ in the assemblies of the church* ... by his Spirit, accompanying all ordinances of worship with a gracious, divine efficacy, evidencing itself by blessed operations on the minds and hearts of the congregation ... (5) To *their preservation in faith*, love and fruitfulness ...

3. *The administration of the seals of the covenant* is committed unto them, as the stewards of the house of Christ ...

4. It is incumbent on them *to preserve the truth or doctrine of the gospel* ...

5. It belongs unto their charge and office, diligently *to labour for the conversion of souls unto God* ...

6. It belongs unto men ... to be *ready, willing, and able, to comfort, relieve, and refresh, those that are tempted,* tossed, wearied with fears and grounds of disconsolation, in times of trial and desertion ... Amongst them there are some always that are cast under darkness and disconsolation in a peculiar manner: some at the entrance of their conversion unto God, whilst they have a deep sense of the terror of the Lord, the sharpness of conviction, and the uncertainty of their condition; some are relapsed into sin or omissions of duties; some under great, sore and lasting

afflictions; some upon pressing, urgent, particular *occasions*; some on sovereign, divine *desertions*; some through the *buffetings of Satan* and the injection of blasphemous thoughts into their minds ... It belongs unto the office and duty of pastors, -

(1) To be able *rightly to understand the various cases that will occur of this kind* ... A skill, understanding and experience, in the whole nature of the work of the Spirit of God on the souls of men, of the conflict that is between the flesh and the Spirit, of the methods and wiles of Satan, of the wiles of principalities and powers or wicked spirits, of the nature and effects and ends, of divine desertions, with wisdom to ... fit medicines and remedies unto every sore and distemper, are required hereunto ...

(2) To be ready and willing to *attend unto the especial cases that may be brought unto them* ...

(3) To *bear patiently and tenderly with the weakness*, ignorance, dullness, slowness to believe and receive satisfaction, yea, it may be, impertinencies, in them that are so tempted ...

In the discharge of the whole pastoral office, there is not anything of duty that is of more importance, nor wherein the Lord Jesus Christ is more concerned ... than this is ...

7. A *compassionate suffering* with all the members of the church in all their trials and troubles ...

8. *Care of the poor* and *visitation of the sick* are parts of this duty, commonly known, though commonly neglected ...

11. That ... without which all the rest will neither be useful unto men nor be accepted with the great Shepherd, Christ Jesus ... is, *a humble, holy exemplary conversation, in all godliness and honesty.*[1]

III

It was, I think, James Moffatt who spoke of 'the dark grey pool of Owen's ratiocination;' and, whoever it was, the phrase

1 *John Owen, Works*, ed. William H. Goold (London: Banner of Truth Trust, 1968), XVI: pp. 74-89.

is a perfect fit. Owen's laborious sentence structure and his preference for matter-of-fact words that lack colour makes him perhaps the least attractive of Puritan writers. Anyone attuned to the lively rhetoric of today will always find reading Owen to be a demanding exercise. But in analytical precision, thoroughness and weight, even at the cost of some redundancy, Owen stands supreme. My slimmed-down reproduction above of his account of pastoral duty indicates the magisterial quality of his mind, and though his style is academic and cool, what he says has an authenticity that reflects the years in pastoral ministry (at Fordham and Coggeshall) with which his public ministry began. Nor is he at any point out of the Puritan mainstream. This can be seen by comparing his survey with the outline of chapter 2, 'The Oversight of the Flock,' in Richard Baxter's *Reformed Pastor*, as laid out on the contents pages of William Brown's edition of the work. Baxter wrote in 1656, Owen some thirty years later, but the correspondence in thought is remarkable.

The Oversight of the Flock

Section 1: The Nature of this Oversight

This Oversight extends to all the Flock

1. We must labour for the conversion of the unconverted.
2. We must give advice to inquirers who are under conviction of sin.
3. We must study to build up those who are already partakers of divine grace.
4. We must exercise a careful oversight of families.
5. We must be diligent in visiting the sick.
6. We must be faithful in reproving and admonishing offenders.
7. We must be careful in exercising Church discipline.

Section 2: The Manner of this Oversight

The Ministerial Work must be carried on

1. Purely for God, and the salvation of souls.
2. Diligently and laboriously.
3. Prudently and orderly.
4. Insisting chiefly on the greatest and most necessary things.
5. With plainness and simplicity.
6. With humility.
7. With a mixture of severity and mildness.
8. With seriousness, earnestness and zeal.
9. With tender love to our people.
10. With patience.
11. With reverence.
12. With spirituality.
13. With earnest desires and expectations of success.
14. Under a deep sense of our own insufficiency and of our dependence on Christ.
15. In unity with other ministers.

Section 3: The Motives to this Oversight

1. From the relation in which we stand to the flock – we are overseers.
2. From the efficient cause of this relation – the Holy Ghost.
3. From the dignity of the object which is committed to our charge – the Church of God.
4. From the price paid for the Church – which he hath purchased with his blood.[2]

---

2 *Richard Baxter, The Reformed Pastor*, ed. William Brown (Edinburgh: Banner of Truth Trust, 1974), pp. 28-29.

John Owen and Richard Baxter disagreed on some secondary matters relating to the organising of churches in the England of their day and the exact stating of the doctrine of God's grace, but on the ideal of pastoral ministry, as the above extracts show, they saw in effect eye to eye. For both of them, the presbyteral vocation was the living out of a sustained and all-absorbing dedication to the love and service of a holy, gracious, sovereign God and of needy people to whom the presbyter must reach out as God's commissioned agent. The pastor should see himself as a man set apart to preach Bible truth, to teach Christ and to counsel the spiritually perplexed by the light of the written Word; to convert, nurture, watch over and care for sinners; to pray for them, bring wisdom to them, model godliness before them, and lead them into and in doxology, fidelity, purity, humility, maturity, and joy in Christ; and to fight in whatever way particular situations might require for the fullness and forthrightness of the faith. I began this Epilogue by asking: can the church survive without pastors of this quality today, fulfilling their ministry according to Puritan specifications? I leave my readers to ponder this question as now I close.[3]

3 The following, from Owen p. 89, written in the 1680s, merits thought: 'The present ruin of religion, as unto its power, beauty and glory, in all places, ariseth principally from this cause, that multitudes of those who undertake this office [i.e. become pastors] are neither in any measure fit for it, nor do either conscientiously attend unto or diligently perform the duties that belong unto it. It ever was and ever will be true in general, "Like priest, like people."'

Other Christian Focus titles that may be of interest ...

Puritan Profiles

54 Contemporaries of the Westminster Assembly

WILLIAM BARKER

ISBN 978-1-85792-191-5

The history of seventeenth century England was tumultuous. During this period England underwent a civil war, a regicide, an experiment with republican government, a restoration of monarchy and constant upheavals in politics and religion. What a confusing period! As the century began Puritans were poised against Episcopalians, parliament against the forces of an absolutist monarchy and the question hung in the air – what kind of Christian expression would the Church of England eventually reflect?

Will Barker's love of biography, historian's eye for detail, his personal devotion to Christ and Scripture make these pages an expertly guided tour of the varied characters and remarkable personalities drawn together by the Westminster Assembly.

Sinclair B. Ferguson,
Senior Minister, First Presbyterian Church, Columbia, South Carolina

William Barker is Professor of Church History, Emeritus at Westminster Theological Seminary, Philadelphia, Pennsylvania.

18 Words

The most important words you will ever know

J.I. Packer

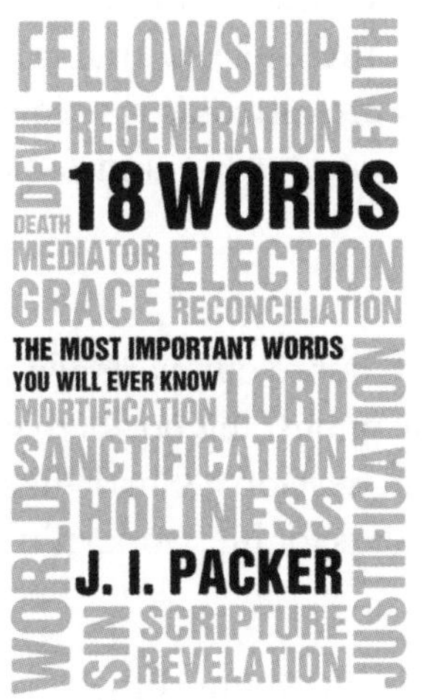

ISBN 978-1-84550-327-7

If the modern world can be characterised by one thing it is probably the enormous increase in the number of words around – but that increase has also been accompanied by a seemingly corresponding decrease in understanding. It is the irony of the information age that instead of bringing clarity it has raised uninformed opinion to the same level as truth.

The church has also not been faultless. Rather than discuss ideas in order to come to some settled agreement, the church has been characterised as trying to make words mean different things in order to accommodate differences.

But the church should be a beacon of light to the world. The church has the words of eternal life.

J. I. Packer is a master wordsmith. He is also gifted with the ability of showing where truth lies in complicated reasoning. These skills combine to make Words from God a fascinating read – and a life-changing one.

The 18 words are:

Death	Holiness	Regeneration
Devil	Justification	Revelation
Election	Lord	Sanctification
Faith	Mediator	Scripture
Fellowship	Mortification	Sin
Grace	Reconciliation	World.

Christian Focus Publications

publishes books for all ages

Our mission statement –

STAYING FAITHFUL
In dependence upon God we seek to impact the world through literature faithful to His infallible Word, the Bible. Our aim is to ensure that the LORD Jesus Christ is presented as the only hope to obtain forgiveness of sin, live a useful life and look forward to heaven with Him.

REACHING OUT
Christ's last command requires us to reach out to our world with His gospel. We seek to help fulfil that by publishing books that point people towards Jesus and help them develop a Christ-like maturity. We aim to equip all levels of readers for life, work, ministry and mission.

Books in our adult range are published in three imprints.

Christian Focus contains popular works including biographies, commentaries, basic doctrine and Christian living. Our children's books are also published in this imprint.

Mentor focuses on books written at a level suitable for Bible College and seminary students, pastors, and other serious readers. The imprint includes commentaries, doctrinal studies, examination of current issues and church history.

Christian Heritage contains classic writings from the past.

Christian Focus Publications Ltd,
Geanies House, Fearn, Ross-shire,
IV20 1TW, Scotland, United Kingdom,
info@christianfocus.com
www.christianfocus.com